MW01120674

To Neville!

Who is a true

Business CHIEF!

Thanks for all your

support. ☺

Barbara

Meetings in Moccasins

Leadership with wisdom and maturity

BARBARA WITTMANN

Icons in interior were created by Gabi Loferer

Cover and author photos were created by Dirk Belling – www.belling-marketing.de

Translation from the German language edition: Meetings in Mokassins by Barbara Wittmann Copyright © Springer Fachmedien Wiesbaden 2013 Springer Fachmeden is part of Springer Science+Business Media. All Rights Reserved

Balboa Press books may be ordered through booksellers or by contacting:

Balboa Press
A Division of Hay House
1663 Liberty Drive
Bloomington, IN 47403
www.balboapress.com
1 (877) 407-4847

Print information available on the last page.

ISBN: 978-1-5043-3323-8 (sc)
ISBN: 978-1-5043-3322-1 (hc)
ISBN: 978-1-5043-3321-4 (e)

Library of Congress Control Number: 2015909542

Balboa Press rev. date: 06/19/2015

For all brave leaders walking their talk
and wanting to make a difference

CONTENTS

THE SYMBOLS

Interview with a modern chief: These are the voices of people who have distinguished themselves by extraordinary entrepreneurship or innovative ideas. The excerpts come from our personal conversations.

Your medicine bag: Fill your personal medicine bag that will remind you which values are the sources of your personal strength.

Your medicine walk: Here, you will walk the path to your own personal answers to a specific topic.

The Chief: Here, the chief shows you the connection between old Native American wisdom and modern business.

ACKNOWLEDGMENTS

Thank you from the bottom of my heart to all the people who enrich my life and nurture my soul.

Bernadette Wittmann – Thank you for believing in my dreams long before they became tangible to others.

Gabi Loferer – Thank you for giving my words wings with your images. Thank you for creating all graphics in this book. (www.visualmutation.de)

Karen Christine Angermayer – Thank you for your word art, which helped shape the soul of this book. (www.worte-die-wirken.de)

Elvira Kretschmer – Thank you for reminding me time and again of the cycle of letting go and starting new.

Ute Küffner – Thank you for inspiring me to work as a coach. The work has filled my life with joy.

Theo Knaus – Thank you for living the gifts of the vision quest and for inspiring me with it.

Sabina Wyss – Thank you for opening new spaces for life and soul.

Meredith Little – Thank you for the conversations and deeply shared thoughts, which have nurtured and carried many aspects of this book.

Gigi Coyle – Thank you for creating space for new experiences and for your passion for council that inspired me, too.

Sabine Asgodom – Thank you for motivating me to write this book.

Christina Huber – Thank you for your straightforward Bavarian honesty and for your clear words when I had doubts.

Katja Rück and Merle – Than you for a new perspective on communities and how they are created.

Sabrina Oberortner, Brigitte Weber, Viola Cester, Susanne Hache, Claus Pflug, Sabine Faltmann – Thank you for allowing me to live my dream of a sustainable work community with you.

Katja Blum – Thank you for you heartfelt translation and help to bring this book to the United States and other English-speaking countries

Walking Thunder – Thank you for your laughter, guidance, and support. Your blessing to publish this book in your home country means a lot to me. May the teaching continue …

I would also like to thank the people who took time to talk to me and allowed their experiences to be part of this book. I am very grateful to:

Prof. Dr. Claus Hipp
HiPP GmbH & Co.Vertrieb KG, www.hipp.de

Antje von Dewitz
VAUDE Sport GmbH & Co. KG, www.vaude.com

Jon Christoph Berndt®
brandamazing GmbH, www.brandamazing.com

Semiha Sander
EBS Universität für Wirtschaft und Recht gGmbH, www.ebs.edu

Gaby Just
JUST PURE GmbH, www.justpure.de

Ute Küffner
Essence Leadership, www.essenceleadership.com

Theo Knaus
Knaus Consulting, www.knaus-consulting.ch

Meredith Little
School of Lost Borders, www.schooloflostborders.org

Felix Finkbeiner
Plant-for-the-Planet, www.plant-for-the-planet.org

Prof. Dr. Christian Berg
German Association for the Club of Rome, www.clubofrome.de

INTRODUCTION
A CHILDHOOD HERO GOES BUSINESS

Stories and legends of Native Americans have intrigued most of us from a very young age. Squanto and the Pilgrims, the tales of Chingachgook and Hawkeye, Hiawatha and the Great Peacemaker, Sitting Bull. They were heroes, strong and courageous, defying danger and fighting the good fight—even giving their lives if necessary.

Today, we see the Indian chief as an embodiment of wisdom, experience, calm, clarity, pride, and courage. A chief is a leader who guides his tribe safely on life's journey. A man who has his people's trust, no matter what. A man with natural authority and vision, who knows each and every member of his tribe, with all their strengths and weaknesses. A man who possesses the very qualities we would like to see in our corporate business leaders.

Native American culture is alive and growing in the United States, and the traditions of the North American tribal nations are still a vital part of that culture. Native Americans today place the teachings of their elders into a new, modern context, drawing from them the strength and inspiration needed to face the challenges of life in the twenty-first century.

I would like to open up that source of strength and inspiration to the readers of this book. I would like to build a bridge between old and new, translate things into a contemporary context. I honor Native American wisdom and traditions. I am grateful that these traditions enrich our world to this day. And I know that not everybody in his or her native country sees it that way.

I am sharing these things with you here in deepest gratitude and in the knowledge that the subject is much broader and deeper than I will be able to express in these pages. This book is a beginning—the beginning of a journey that I started by buying a teepee.

Seven years ago, I fulfilled a childhood dream and bought an authentic teepee. The full-size tent became an important haven for me, a place where I was able to leave my hectic job as an IT consultant and coach behind to reflect and recharge. At that time, I began to learn all I could about Native Americans. I read countless books about them and traveled to their homelands in the United States. Later, I participated in workshops in Europe and the United States. I had the chance to learn from wonderful people, and I am still going on regular vision quests in the wilderness to get back in touch with myself and stay connected to the old teachings.

I was fortunate enough to meet Native medicine men and women, although I was never formally trained in their traditions. My greatest teacher is and has always been nature. The things I read and learned in the workshops did not really sink in until I spent time alone in wild places that were untouched by man. More and more, I felt that it was necessary to transfer the things I was learning to the modern business world. Today, we need nothing more than naturalness.

Native American teachings and IT? At first glance, these two things seem about as compatible as fire and water. And that was my problem throughout the last few years. How was I supposed to bring these two worlds together, both of which held so much fascination for me, yet were so fundamentally different?

In many ways, writing this book was an act of courage, just like my last vision quest in the summer of 2012, where I was confronted with the wind, cold, rain, dust, and rattlesnakes of the Californian Inyo Mountains. Working on this book meant questioning my own business life and that of the people around me with whom I am dealing every day. And it also took courage to bring my truth into the world.

The fact that I needed to do it anyway was confirmed for me in a chance meeting on a hike at Point Reyes in California on New Year's Eve 2012.

I still had a long way ahead of me, and I bought a map. I got to talking to a ranger who told me that this was her last day on the job after twelve years. I asked her what she had learned, what her key takeaway was after twelve years of service preserving nature.

"Integration," was her answer. "It's not enough," she said, "to lead people into nature. We need to integrate the rules of nature into our everyday life in order to create real change in the world."

Suddenly, I understood that her words were the essence of this book. That all my travels over the years, all my searching and finding, had been leading me to this point: integrating the knowledge of the connectedness of nature, its rhythms and growth cycles, as well as its protective mechanisms and power of survival into our lives. Not just into our personal lives, but also very strongly into our professional lives, which, for many people, have turned into hamster wheels they can only escape through illness or inner resignation.

What would an Indian chief of old have to say to us today? How would he behave in our business world? Where would his ways get him in trouble? Which positive things would he bring to the table? What would he change? How do we recognize through the image of the Indian chief what our true objectives are, why we are here, and how we can best *serve*? Based on these thoughts, I wrote this book for you. Clearly, the Indian chief in these pages is an image, a composite character expressing the wisdom of nature and certain Native American traditions. He is certainly not a straight depiction of modern Native American life or Native business leaders: he is the chief.

My fervent hope is that the chief you are going to meet in the following pages will encourage you to think about some things and inspire you to be more mindful with yourself, your surroundings, and nature. In business and in your personal life—ultimately, they are the same.

A-ho!

Another important note: of course this book is meant for both male and female business leaders. The archetype of the chief is a metaphor for men and women who have achieved a state of internal and external balance, wisdom, and maturity, regardless of their gender.

In many native cultures, women are just as aware of their skills, strengths, and value as men are. Neither would even think of being a rival of the other. Both roles are equally valid; both are necessary to keep the powers in a community in balance and ensure the survival of the entire tribe.

PART 1
The Chief

CHAPTER 1

Warbonnet and HR: How Do You Recognize a True Chief?

The doors of the glass elevators slide open without a sound. Two young men and a young woman exit and walk down the hallway, which is decorated in elegant shades of gray, to the Human Resources office.

All three are in their mid-twenties and wear suits that are expensive enough to look unassuming. Their shoes have leather soles, and their hair is perfectly coiffed. All three carry portfolios and iPads. There is no doubt that these three feel that their success is a done deal, even though their careers have barely begun.

Behind the three, another person stepped out of the elevator and is now following them about a step behind. He looks different and is significantly older, although it is difficult to guess his age. His long, open hair is black with gray streaks. He obviously has Native American roots, because he wears traditional native clothes: tan trousers and shirt, both embellished with colorful embroidery. On his head, he wears a warbonnet, a feathered headdress of the kind seen in movies.

The three young adults do not realize that the Native American man has entered the HR office with them. They are too wrapped up in their own things.

The office is occupied by a middle-aged man. His head is drooping slightly, just like the plants on the windowsill behind him. He doesn't have a lot of time. Application portfolios are piled high on his desk. It is always the same. The same portfolios. Same phrases. Same lives. And they all want the same: a lot of money.

The man rubs his face and examines the four candidates now sitting before him. He is not entirely sure what he is looking for. He is not a trained HR representative. This job was just piled on top of the others. He is really the head of the international business unit. As if that wasn't enough work. He doesn't even dare to think about all the things still on the agenda today. *And who invited the Indian?* He has seen a lot of strange applicants, but this guy in his Halloween costume tops them all!

"Is it October already?" The HR rep tries to open the conversation with a joke. The Indian gives him a piercing look. He does not smile back at the tired man. The two young men and the woman laugh. Surely, the Indian is already out, just due to his his silly outfit. This just increased their own chances to get the job from 25 percent to 33.33 percent.

All right, let's get this over with, the HR guy thinks. *In half an hour, I need to be at the board meeting.* Aloud, he says, "I have three questions for you, and you each get fifteen seconds to answer each question. Question one." He looks at the four applicants. "Why do you think you are the right person for the job?" He nods at candidate one.

Candidate one is very confident, because he practiced at home in front of the mirror. "I am an expert in strategy development, strategic sourcing, and IT management. My focus is on smart-sourcing, outsourcing, offshoring, and business-process redesign. I studied abroad for a year and am fluent in French and Spanish. And I am convinced that my skills are a perfect match for your company."

Candidate two clears his throat. Should he try to come up with something else on the fly? He decides against it, because fifteen seconds is not a long time. "I am an expert in strategy development, strategic sourcing, and IT management. My focus is on smart-sourcing, outsourcing, offshoring, and business-process redesign. I studied abroad for a year and am fluent in French and Spanish. And Chinese," he adds importantly. "And, of course, I am also convinced that my skills are a perfect match for your company."

Candidate three, the young woman, seems a little unsure. But then she says, "I am an expert in strategy development, strategic sourcing, and IT management. My focus is on smart-sourcing, outsourcing, offshoring, and business-process redesign. I studied abroad for *two years* and am fluent in French, Spanish, and Chinese. And Russian," she adds importantly. "And I, too, am convinced that my skills are a perfect match for your company. I'm also unmarried and don't have children, so I would be available to work at any time." Someone told her that this is a very important point for female applicants.

Nodding, the two young men raise their hands and say, "Same here." They don't have children and can work around the clock.

The HR guy does not give any indication regarding whether or not he liked the three answers. Instead, he looks at the Indian, who says just three words: "I am chief."

Confused, the HR guy clears his throat and continues. "Question two. If you get the job, what would you change in this company? What personal mark would you put on our house?"

Quick like a shot, candidate one answers, "Minimize costs!"

"Strategic realignment!" exclaims candidate two.

Candidate three responds calmly, "Outsourcing."

The Indian says, "I am chief. I want my tribe to be happy. Only a happy tribe remains strong for many generations and brings in a good harvest."

The three young people laugh. This guy is completely off his rocker!

The HR guy thinks, *Maybe I should suggest to the board that we calculate the numbers for the next quarter in bushels of corn harvested instead of dollars.* But he remains inscrutable. "Last question," he says. "The company goes bankrupt. Let's hope not. That is why we are hiring *you*, after all. But who do you hold responsible?"

"Well, Controlling, of course," says candidate one with a triumphant smile.

Nodding, candidate two adds, "And heads will certainly roll in Sales."

Also nodding, candidate three says, "Well, apart from those two departments, HR certainly has some responsibility!"

She closes her mouth quickly, recognizing from the look the HR guy gives her that her answer wasn't quite appropriate.

The Indian says, "I am chief. I am responsible."

The HR guy nods, makes a note, and gets up. "Thank you very much, lady and gentlemen. That is all."

Surprised, the three young people jump to their feet. "But I've got a—" all three exclaim at the same time, opening their portfolios and iPads, wanting to show their certificates and short presentations.

The HR guy declines. "Thank you very much. I'll call, if I need anything else from you." Then he turns to the Indian. "Uh, how can I reach you? I suppose you don't have a cell phone." He utters the term *cell phone* very slowly, as if wanting to teach the Indian a new word.

The Indian looks at the HR guy for a long time. His lashes don't even twitch. "I will be there when you call me."

* * *

Admittedly, such an interview has never happened and, most likely, will never happen. Fact is that many young leaders come from elite schools with big names and are going to interviews armed with a stack of awards and international certificates that might be very impressive but don't say anything about their true leadership abilities.

They have collected vast stores of knowledge, some of them in record time. And they deserve full respect for that. They worked hard and received their reward: the diploma. But what they didn't automatically acquire is maturity—maturity of the spirit, heart, and soul.

This is not the young applicants' fault but has a different root cause. It starts much earlier, with the fact that our society does not have rituals anymore that make a man out of a boy, a woman out of a girl, a chief out of a warrior, a manager out of an Ivy League graduate. Even the transition from teenager to young adult does not get any space in the system of our lives. There is nobody to show the young people how it is done, which phase is ending and which new phase is about to begin.

How do we test when a student is mature enough to be a young professional and when a young professional can call himself a manager—and has earned the title instead of getting it instantly, like magic—because they were printing new business cards anyway?

Let us leave our three young, hopeful, high-potential applicants from the interview for a moment and look at the portfolio of a chief. What is a chief, what are his characteristics, and how does he learn the skills of a true leader whose decisions inspire the trust of an entire tribe that will gladly follow him—in good times and bad?

If an Indian chief were to submit a job application, it could look like this:

> **My Brother in the HR Department of the Company-Reaching-for-the-Stars!**
>
> You are looking for an experienced chief for your tribe.
>
> Today, I am following my inner voice and would like to offer you my services and wisdom.
>
> As you know, a warrior must go through many trials before he can call himself a chief. He must push himself to the limits of his body, spirit, and heart—and sometimes beyond them. He needs to plunge into his own depths and find the place in the world that only he can occupy.
>
> In the course of many years, he is also taught the skills of a good warrior, but it is really his soul that matures during this time. A good warrior

learns that it is not enough to know how to carve an arrow but when to shoot it and when to leave it in his quiver.

When a warrior is made chief, he has met everything he is: his strength and his love, his talents and his skills, but also his pride, his fear, and his stubbornness. No life situations would surprise him, because he knows how he reacts to them and how he can harness his emotions and actions to lead to a solution that will be good for all involved—for a chief also knows that everything in the world is connected.

Therefore, he will never make a decision that furthers only his own interests or those of individual members of the tribe, but will ensure that it will benefit all brothers and sisters. And his decision comes from his heart, never just from his mind. Once the decision is made, the chief will keep his word and never waver.

A chief bears full responsibility for his tribe. No tribe member will ever be judged or punished for doing something that is rooted in the thoughts and actions of the chief.

A good chief is just as skilled in waging war as he is in lighting the peace pipe. He knows when it is time to advance and when it is better to withdraw. He respects nature and her four elements: fire, water, earth, and air. From them, he learns about the cycles of life, which inform his decisions every day. He knows that there is a time for sowing, growing, and reaping—and a time for regeneration.

A chief is unafraid, even as the world around him is frightened. He knows that we do not fear the event itself but its consequences. Yet the consequences of the event—the true core of our fears—are unknown until they occur and can be changed. That is why a chief is unafraid.

The chief also knows when it is time to die. When that time comes, he will leave without you having to find a reason to make him. The chief knows when to step aside to make room for the birth of something new. He will stand tall and walk away happy because he knows that he has given everything in his heart and his power.

My brother, my warbonnet contains twenty-four feathers. Each feather stands for a great victory and great courage. As you know, not every chief owns such a magnificent warbonnet. Some earn only two or three feathers in the course of their lives. And my medicine bag, the leather pouch I carry with me, contains a snail shell and a feather. The shell reminds me that it is better to walk slowly than too fast and that there are times when I need to withdraw to make up my mind in peace. And the feather is a reminder to soar into the air and look at everything with the eyes of an eagle, if I want to find the solution to a problem.

> My brother, with happiness and pride, I am offering you my services today. I am prepared to lead your tribe through all tribulations of the coming days.
>
> The Chief

What does this letter show us? It shows that a chief

- brings his entire personality and his whole being to the table, not just studies and theoretical knowledge;
- thinks not just of his own advantage, but of the benefits for the entire company; and
- doesn't apply for a job because of a high-profile job description and big compensation, but because he knows that this is his *place in the world*, where he can make a contribution no other applicant could.

Of course, a letter like the one above would not make it past the first cut in today's business world (although—who knows?).

And yet, there is a connection between the level of our current everyday business life and the values that were lived successfully in Native American tradition.

We are going to look at each of these values in the course of this book and compare them to the modern business world. At the same time, we are going to find out how these values can be established in the business world with simple measures and impulses and how they form the foundation for a healthy corporate culture and sustainable success.

Exercise

Before you continue reading, please select a small bag or pouch. In the course of this book, this pouch will become your personal medicine bag.

What Is a Medicine Bag?

A medicine bag is a small pouch (a leather pouch, in Native American tradition). It is filled with symbols that are important to us, because they stand for our unique characteristics and talents or remind us how to handle certain situations successfully. Native Americans would say that the contents of this pouch are our personal "medicine," like the snail shell and feather in the chief's medicine bag. Clients who fill their medicine bag for the first time as part of my coaching often tell me about its lasting impact on their professional and personal lives.

Your Personal Warbonnet

Now, please take out a piece of paper. We are going to create your personal warbonnet. Please note, in short sentences or keywords, in which situations you

- have shown great courage in your professional or personal life;
- have managed to lead seemingly irreconcilable parties to a satisfactory solution;

- have confronted other people with your truth and prevailed, even though the whole world seemed to be against you; and
- have kept your word and modeled the behavior you expect from your subordinates.

Please feel free to write down other successes or skills you can think of.

Write down this list and use it to fashion your imaginary warbonnet. Display the list in a place where you can easily see it.

Internalize your successes and your apparent failures, which make up your unique personality. Place your medicine bag in the same spot or carry it with you, to the next meeting, for example. A medicine bag and warbonnet help a Native American with finding his courage in times of doubt and remind him of his uniqueness. Harness that power!

And if you are the HR guy: In your next interview, take a moment to imagine what the warbonnet of the candidate would look like, if he had one. Is it a magnificent headdress that speaks of great courage and maturity or does it contain just a few scant downs?

And then choose well.

CHAPTER 2

Lived Values: Walk Your Talk

The conference table is a gleaming oval of black, exotic wood. On the mirror-polished tabletop sit simple white cups and the ubiquitous dry cookies.

The participants of the meeting are just as ubiquitous—men and women in impeccably tailored suits. People entering the room greet the others curtly or not at all. Suddenly, the door opens, and an Indian chief enters the room. We know him from the interview. So he really made it and got the job?

Nobody knows how he did it. There are rumors that this might be a trick of the new consultants who have been sneaking around the company for a few weeks. Or is he even one of the consultants who put on a costume to play Indian chief? Nobody knows. And nobody knows how long he will stay, the man with the long, black hair, who calls himself "The Chief."

He sits down, and his magnificent headdress takes up a lot of space. The men to his left and right need to make room for him. One by one, The Chief looks at every person in the room. His gaze is deep and calm. He gives each person a nod before his gaze moves on to the next. Some people are uncomfortable and look away. Others are curious. A young woman smiles. The gaze of The Chief remains unchanged, regardless of his counterpart's reaction. He gives his full attention to the head of department, who has stood up from his chair to project several slides on the wall. They display words like *competence, efficiency, strategy, sustainability*, and *credibility*.

You look tired, my brother, The Chief thinks, while listening closely. *You are trying to sound successful and strong, but your voice is breaking, and I can see from your erratic hand movements how nervous you are. You know that your success depends on figures, but you have no idea how you could every reach those figures. You want your people to trust you, so you keep pretending that everything is fine. But nothing is as it should be, my brother. Nothing.*

The head of department catches The Chief's eye. He stops, smiles uncertainly, and addresses him directly.

"Would you like to add anything to these points, Chief? What do you think we can do to earn our customers' lasting confidence?"

The Chief thinks for a while.

"Walk your talk," he says after a pause that seems like an eternity to the non-Native Americans. Three of the people at the table have already sent important e-mails and texts on their iPhones and iPads, checked the Dow, and adjusted their portfolios.

"Ah, I'm not sure what you mean," says the head of department.

"Walk your talk," The Chief repeats. His face does not show what he thinks about the man. "It means living the things you say." He pauses to look at every single person at the table. Again, some avert their eyes; some are curious or nervous. The young woman smiles.

The Chief continues, "Your tribe and your customers can sense it if you do not keep your word. And they can also sense it if each of your words is true and comes from your heart. They know it because they can see it in the way you make your decisions. If you know yourself and your values, you can make your decisions quickly and easily. You stand by the things you say and do. You can explain and justify your decisions to your tribe and your customers. Your tribe, your customers and partners know that you stand by your word, whatever happens. And you will only choose employees, customers, and partners who fit in with your values. And you know exactly when you have part with people and things and offers that do not suit you. Sometimes you make decisions of the kind that not everybody would make. But they're your decisions, and if you know your values and your decisions are born from these values, they will be good. Then you walk your talk."

The Chief looks around the room. Everybody is listening intently. Nobody would even think of sending a text message at this moment. The words of the Indian resonate in the minds of listeners. Not everybody is sure that they understood everything, but the core of the message has reached them all.

* * *

Walking your talk is the backbone of the company and its leadership; it's the framework, the guideline for all employees. It means that the company and all employees walk tall and strong through all the trials and challenges of everyday business life, beaming, with pride and joy. Corporate phenomena such as slip-streamers and free-riders, in terms of people and products, are unnecessary, because the employees are all living their values and drawing their ideas from them.

Walking your talk also means that the leader must always be visible, touchable, and approachable for the tribe. In my work as a corporate consultant, I often see chiefs who give their tribe difficult tasks, only to vanish into thin air. That is not the way.

And it also means simply leaving things better than you found them. That the year ends better than it began. Finish every workday with a better feeling than you started with. De-escalate deadlocked meetings with a smile, bring the conflict to another level, and make it possible for all players to take the next step with dignity.

Theo Knaus is a man who is already following this path successfully. I met him on my first vision quest in Colorado. Still deeply moved by our travel experience, we meet on a regular basis to share our experiences in the corporate wilderness. About a year ago, Theo left an upper-management position in a Swiss company to become a freelance consultant specializing in "value-based corporate leadership."

He says, "If the people in the company agree on the values and their realization, it creates trust, familiarity, community, and respect. And even love! So many things we human beings need in order to develop a healthy way. And these things generate power for the individual and power for the entire company."

Sometimes it takes a little while for a company to find and implement its values: for instance, if a family-run company is handed over to the next generation.

Antje von Dewitz, CEO of VAUDE, a renowned manufacturer of outdoor equipment, is a woman who needed to find her way—and did it with great success. It was impossible for her to emulate the leadership style of her father, who founded and shaped the company. So she needed to develop her own style. As a woman. As an entrepreneur. As a mother of four children.

A sign in the VAUDE lobby says "Unternehmen Familie" ("Corporate Family"). Since the foundation of the company, all employees have been on a first-name basis. A culture of trust has been established over decades, which needs to be upheld and nurtured. Every year, the entire company celebrates several parties and events, which brings everybody closer together. In her everyday business life, Antje von Dewitz keeps in touch with her base.

I am a little early for our appointment and decide to wait in the café next to the VAUDE Outlet. While I am wondering why I just bought a third tent next door, even though I don't need one, I spot Antje von Dewitz in the middle of the lunch rush. I like that about her; she's always in the thick of things. When we meet officially in her office, my first impression is confirmed.

Antje von Dewitz is authentic. She is someone I would take on a mountain-climbing tour. Someone you can trust right away.

I am surprised how consistently a company of this size is practicing its values. How authentic and available she is as a leader. She is very close to her tribe: she conducts employee surveys on a regular basis, analyzes them, and creates personality profiles for her managers to record all of their strengths. It is nice to see how authentic leadership, as she calls it, works in the business environment.

The Navajo have a phrase that sums it up: "The Beauty Way."

The Beauty Way means being one with everything: people, things, nature … we are connected to everything and everything is connected to us. The Beauty Way is the deep conviction that everything is influenced by everything else. That even with small things, you can accomplish big things. Thank you can do something good every day. This doesn't have to be a huge business deal; it could be a good personal conversation.

If the leader embodies the Beauty Way, she radiates beauty inside and out. She lives her values effortlessly and naturally. She is a true example, not just in business matters but also on an ethical and spiritual level. She is the embodiment of the things we long for deep in our souls: beauty and perfection in every conversation, every thought, every emotion, every action, every person—and even in every product and service that offer true added value and a service to mankind.

Something for your medicine bag: What are the values you stand for? Which one of them could you make a priority in your company next month? Put a symbol of this value in your medicine bag.

I would like to tell you about another very effective tool: the medicine walk.

A medicine walk means taking a break in nature—perhaps with a conscious, purposeful walk of fifteen or thirty minutes. Begin your walk with a question and let nature be your guide. Take in nature with all senses. By the way, taking a break means that your phone stays home. This is *your* time!

Perhaps you notice a bird or find a beautiful rock. Take the rock home with you. Write down the things you notice while watching the bird. It can also be something as simple as a paper clip that reminds you of something. After every medicine walk, make brief notes of what happened. Which thoughts came to you? Which insights?

There is a sign in Waipiu Valley on the Hawaiian Big Island, the valley where the chiefs used to live. It says: "The land is chief, man is the servant."

Land is chief. Let it teach you! Let nature be your guide. And take your first medicine walk today!

Results of your medicine walk, with the subject "My Values":

CHAPTER 3

Living Your Dreams: When Your Life's Vision Becomes Part of Your Actions

Today's meeting is a small one. The room is the same, as are the table, cups, and cookies. And the Indian chief is here, too. By now, people have gotten used to the man with the big, feathered headdress. Individuality has always been a priority of this company. Well, at least on paper. *But now someone finally dares to be different*, some people think when they see The Chief while getting the obligatory morning coffee in the kitchen.

On the agenda today is team motivation. The head of HR hopes to get some fresh ideas from The Chief.

"How do you motivate your people, your tribe, as you say?" He smiles at the Chief. The Chief does not return the smile.

Instead he asks, "What do people here dream of?"

Everybody at the table laughs, except for The Chief. "Well, what do people dream of? More money, of course! And more free time!" say several voices.

The Chief remains calm. "Why do people dream of more money and free time? What do they need more money and free time for?"

The head of HR shrugs. "To drive bigger cars. Build a house. Pay off their loans. Take several vacations every year."

Everybody nods.

The Chief doesn't say anything. He knows these voices from his tribe. The young warriors, who still have a long way to go before becoming chief, have the same answers. They have wishes and dreams born in the now. An expensive stallion now. New hunting equipment now. Being chief now. If their wishes are not fulfilled immediately, they get impatient and even angry.

"I mean, what do their souls dream of?"

Silence around the table. What do they know about the souls of their employees? And do they even want to know? They have enough on their plates as it is. There is no SOP, no inventory number for souls.

The Chief makes such a long pause that people are getting nervous again.

Then he says, "You cannot demand more performance from your tribe if you don't know their dreams. *Motivation* is not an appropriate word, even though it has been used all over the world for years. I am giving you a new word today: *synchronization*."

Synchronization … the people at the table know this word. It has to do with making sure that all their electronic devices can play the same music.

The Chief continues, "Synchronization means to align your personal and professional dreams. Every member of your tribe has a personal dream. And every member of your tribe has a professional dream. Only if every member of your tribe knows his two dreams and if these two dreams are a fit for the dream of your company, then your tribe will give the performance necessary to realize the dream of your company."

"Personal dream, professional dream, alignment, synchronization, dream of the company." People's heads are spinning. They have been to many workshops and done many crazy things, but this is getting ridiculous.

The Chief nods patiently, as if he is reading the thoughts hovering in the air above the table.

"I am going to give you an example," he says. "One member of your tribe wants to buy a new car. For this, he needs to put in a certain amount of work for a certain period of time."

Nods.

"Another one of your tribe does not just want a new car, but a new home for his family. For this, he needs to put in a certain amount of work for a certain period of time."

More nods.

"And a third wants the car and the house and would like to retire in a few years. For this, he, too, needs to put in a certain amount of work for a certain period of time."

"Yeah, until he's blue in the face," someone jokes. Everybody laughs, except for The Chief.

"These are just three people of your tribe," The Chief continues. "And all three have different dreams. This means that these three people wake up differently in the morning. They are different when they come to the office, and they work in different ways. And each of them goes home at night and dreams his dream. Some dreams have become a little more reality in the course of the day. Some have slipped further out of reach. For instance, if the person in your tribe dreams of having less stress, but you tell him that the figures need to increase and that he needs to work more within the same timeframe. Then dreams collide. And dreams that collide destroy each other. They obliterate each other."

Silence. What The Chief is saying sounds suspiciously like the truth.

"Your tribe is dreaming, whether you know it or not. Each and every member of your tribe is moving on his own dream path. Each has a private dream and a professional dream. And only when both dreams exist, truly great things can be created. Only then will the members of your tribe do the best they can do. Only then will you have the *visions* you always talk about."

This message is sinking in, so The Chief moves on quickly.

"But your company has a dream, too. Your company also wakes up in the morning and expects you and all other employees to come and work on its dream. And it closes its doors at night hoping that a part of its dream has been fulfilled."

Silence.

"But if none of you knows all of these dreams, how can they ever come true?"

Now, the people around the table pause for such a long time that it would be easily possible to send several texts and e-mails. None of them do.

Finally, the head of HR asks, "So, now what?"

The Chief asks the young woman sitting next to him, the one who was the only person smiling at the last meeting, to pass out the big sheets of paper in front of her. Each paper shows a big, black circle with the words "Dream Board" underneath.

* * *

Theo Knaus uses a beautiful image to describe dreams. He compares our personal and professional dreams with a star, saying, "Every person and every company has a fixed star. Even if the path to it might not be completely clear, we take a step towards it every day. The closer we get, the stronger is the power of the star. Every individual in the company needs to agree with the company's fixed star. He needs to be able to move closer to it as a person, independent of his job and the corporate leadership. And the star needs to make sense for his personal development, for the soul of each individual. If both fit together, it generates a force that makes extraordinary things possible, because all powers strive for the same goal."

What is your fixed star, how do you find it, and how do you keep your eyes on it? Following, we are going to look at these questions.

The Dream Board: Symbol of Our Professional and Personal Vision

Most of us know by now that it is important to have goals. We also know that it is important not just to know our goals but also to put them into words. This is how we ask our subconscious to pick up all hints, information, and chances that might help us reach our goals.

So, the first step is knowing our goals.

The second step is putting them into words on paper.

In the third step, we intensify the effect by creating a so-called Dream Board.

Background: dreams can only come true if we work on them every day. They shouldn't just flash in our mind from time to time before sinking back into oblivion; we need to let them seep deeply into every fiber of our being. Our mind is happy when we feed it with facts concerning our dream. And our soul rejoices when we *truly feel* our dream. We need to plant the seed of our dream in our soul so that it can grow and one day fill our entire being. Then the facts of our dream become reality.

The Dream Board is about planting that seed to make it grow inside of us. The Dream Board shows the course of our goals in a calendar year.

Ask yourself: What does my dream look like? What is going to happen to it within the next year? And, most importantly, how will I feel when it comes true?

Like the men and women in the meeting with The Chief, you will now create your Dream Board. As with all exercises in this book, I recommend that you try the exercise instead of just reading it. The result will be worth it!

Take a big piece of cardboard. Draw a circle in the middle and divide it into four areas:

1. Myself
2. Customers and business partners
3. Family and friends
4. Role models

Your *dream* is at the center. What is your dream? What is the reason why you get out of bed in the morning and go to work? I mean your real dream—the one behind the daily eight- to twelve-hour workday, the mortgage, the bills and credit card payments. *What is your personal dream?* If you live your dream, it will impact all four segments. The purpose of your Dream Board is to depict these four areas of your life, once they have been touched by the power of your dream. Feelings are very important here.

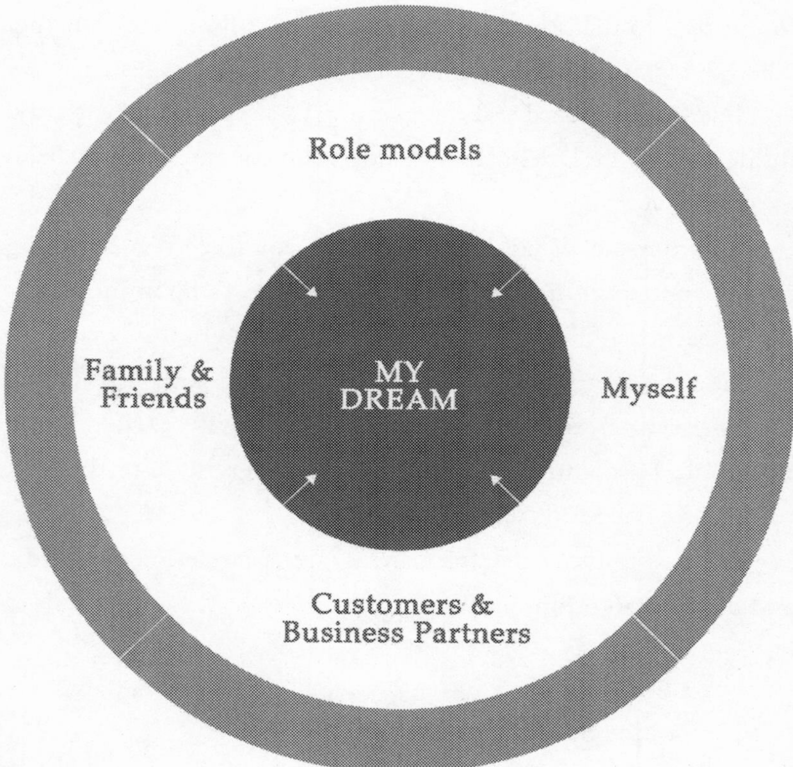

Figure 1: The Dream Board

Creating your personal Dream Board is fun—not just by yourself, but as a team!

Browse magazines for images and captions that would fit in each segment. You don't have to fill the whole Dream Board in one session; it is okay to keep thinking about it and grow it slowly. If you find an image you would like to put in a certain segment even though it doesn't seem to make sense there, glue it to that exact spot. It will make sense to you when the time is right. Don't ask too many questions. Trust your intuition.

Your Dream: Status Quo a Year from Now

As I have said before, the core of your Dream Board is your dream for the next twelve months. Where do you want to be in a year? The clearer your dream is to you, the more power your Dream Board will gain. Please choose only one image for the core. This image or symbol stands for your purpose, your intention, your mission. Right now, your dream core may be empty. That is okay and is just as good and useful as a beginning.

Describe the following next to the image: What is likely to be reality a year from now? How will you feel when all these things happen?

Here is an example from my own Business Dream Board:

> *As a consulting firm, we shape the concept of people-oriented IT. We set new standards for the work environment in this fast-paced industry. We use our expertise in more and more innovative projects, because*

they need a lot of sensitivity, good instincts, and team spirit. Our customers love the creative, unconventional way in which we solve problems.

My feelings:

I am proud to have such wonderful, creative people work with me and for me. I am happy about our good relationships with our customers. I depart from common industry standards in many ways, and the people around me love me for it.

When we burn for our dreams and keep working to make them come true, it has an effect on the people around us. That is why the Dream Board does not just impact our own dream but also serves as an indicator of the things that will happen around us within the year.

Role Models

Everyone has role models: people in our present or from the past, who we admire for their talents or certain personality traits. Admiring someone is a sign that we already have these exact traits inside of us—emerging or still hidden deep inside. When we dare to live our dreams, these characteristics come to light and become part of our everyday life.

Who are your role models, living or dead? Look for pictures of them to add to your Dream Board. Which personality traits and talents of your role models will you emulate in your thoughts and actions when you are living your dream?

Myself

You are the main player in this game of life. What do you want your game- and play board to look like in the future? Find images for this. Who are you when you are living your dream? How do you look; how do you feel? Where do you live, what do you eat, how do you dress? Which things and people surround you?

Customers and Business Partners

Being in the right place at the right time and meeting the right people doesn't happen by accident. It is the natural consequence of your clear goals.

We know this example of clear focus from buying a new car: suddenly, we see it everywhere, and the whole world seems to be driving this car! This is how your conscious and subconscious mind focuses on the realization of your goals and dreams: sharp as a laser.

Who are your ideal customers and business partners? What character traits do they stand for? How do they think, what do they feel, how do they act, and what decisions do they make? And how does the partnership influence you?

Express this information and your feelings in words and images.

Family and Friends

Your family and friends will be your main supporters. Helping you fulfill your dream is also going to impact their lives. You will see that your relationships and friendships gain importance and depth, once your Dream Board starts having an effect.

How will your dream influence your family and loved ones? How will it change or deepen your connections to people when your dream comes true?

Find appropriate images for this as well.

And What Does the Dream Board of Your Team or the One for a Specific Project Look Like?

Invest some time in creating a joint Dream Board. You will be surprised how much faster and more effortless reaching your goals will become when all team members have internalized the Dream Board as the core of their actions. Remember the words of The Chief: "Dreams that collide destroy each other. They obliterate each other." Do you all have the same dream, at least in big parts? Is everybody pulling together? Or are you all pulling on different parts of the rope so that the rope cannot move and just frays over time, while your strength wanes and your efforts cancel each other out?

If you know a little bit about marketing, you know that every brand—cars, detergent, chocolate, or clothing—has a brand core. The leading brands invest a lot of time and money in defining the core of the brand and analyzing every product in light of that core. A product that clashes with the brand core is (ideally) not being produced.

This is what the Dream Board is going to do for your team and for you as a leader.

Every feeling, thought, and action, every decision should be connected to your dream. This is the way to create structure, conclusiveness, efficiency, and effectiveness—all the things we strive for. And this is the way to make sense—for each individual and for the company.

If you are thinking right now that you don't need a Dream Board, because you know what your goals are, and your employees really don't need one, because they are supposed to do what you tell them—then you should definitely do the Dream Board exercise. You will be surprised at the secret dreams that come to light and how the people around you become more motivated work more effectively—on their own development and in completing the tasks of their jobs. As always, this will be reflected in level-headed, committed employees and healthy profit margins.

Something for your medicine bag: What reminds you of your personal dream? Where do you want to be a year from now? Place the symbol in your medicine bag.

Results of your medicine walk, with the subject "My Dream":

CHAPTER 4

Healthy Ego: Giving Yourself and Others Room to Grow

Today, The Chief is sitting in the young woman's office. Their desks touch in the middle. The young woman, Julia, likes this unusual man. Apart from the fact that she thinks he is very handsome, she finds his presence extremely calming. And she is not the only one; wherever The Chief goes, the atmosphere becomes relaxed. People take deep breaths and calm down; heated discussions cool off; conversations become deeper.

"May I ask you something?" Julia asks cautiously. The Chief looks up from his screen. He nods encouragingly.

"How do you manage to get your entire tribe to like and respect you?"

She lowers her voice so that their conversation cannot be overheard out in the hallway through the open door. "I mean, you see what is going on here. Nobody likes the boss, because he is ruthless and just looks out for his own advantage. He pretends that he is the only one deserving praise for the things we do all day. And several times a week, he gives us more work—on top of what we have to do already! Everybody knows that he really doesn't care that we have way too much overtime and have had several burnout cases—as long as he is looking good in the end. Do you get this kind of thing, too?"

The Chief listens attentively. He has a look on his face that she could just enjoy for hours. For the first time since he joined the company, he smiles a little. But then he becomes serious again—much too soon.

"First of all, it is not important that my tribe likes me. It is important that my tribe *trusts* me. And yes, it happens among the young warriors, too. They don't care if a brother is sick or exhausted or if a brother shoots faster and has better aim. And they don't care if the buffalo suffers before it dies. The only goal of these young warriors is to bring down the buffalo. They will never become chief that way. A chief knows his own value. And he knows the value of all others. There comes a day when he realizes that he is not going to be the best and greatest by fighting ruthlessly for being the best and greatest. He can only become the best and greatest in his field if he gives others the chance to become the best and greatest in their field. We reach our goals only as a community. That doesn't mean that we should make ourselves smaller than we are. But it does mean that our ego, as you call it, must be healthy, not sick. Only a healthy ego recognizes itself and others."

* * *

True words. Today, rivalries and territorial attitudes take up a big part of our professional life. A huge amount of energy is wasted on them. What would happen if these struggles didn't happen, if instead, all energy was available for the development of new projects, products, and ideas? What would happen if our egos were healthy?

What Is the "Healthy Ego" The Chief Speaks of?

Much has been written about the ego. It is often compared to or defined as self-confidence. In the original Freudian sense, however, the ego is merely our sense of self, the part of us that knows our conscious mind. In my opinion, this is the difference between an unhealthy and a healthy ego. A person with too strong or too big an ego tends to be very self-centered. Some people say that the term *ego* stands for "edging God out." People who do this are very aware of their own value—being convinced that they have a very high value—and seek only their own advantage. They remain very rigid in their definition of themselves.

My personal view of a healthy ego, which is not based on scientific studies but on observations in my professional and personal life, is this:

A healthy ego is the shift from self-confidence to a sense of self.

If I know who I am and where my place in society is, the *I* turns into *we* without dissolving or losing the *I*.

From a Native American perspective, a healthy ego means that the person has found the center of his own wheel of life. The four shields of his wheel are in balance. We will discuss the wheel of life and its meaning more in-depth later in this book.

When we are truly in balance with ourselves and others, "good old boy" networks, finger-pointing, image neuroses, taking credit for another's work, mobbing, and brown-nosing become obsolete, because:

A person who knows the core of his strength
doesn't need rivalries or territories.

Or, as Theo Knaus puts it succinctly, "A boss who is in balance with himself doesn't need to project his team's success onto himself. He can give credit where credit is due."

In this context, I am reminded of an interesting remark made by Claus Hipp, entrepreneur and the father of the Hipp brand of baby food that has nourished generations of German children. He said a word we don't hear often these days: *humility*. "The courage to serve," as he calls it.

True wealth, he says, is the wealth of the soul. We accumulate material riches, but we cannot take them with us. He wants to use and treat the goods entrusted to him with respect and responsibility and use what he earns to serve and help others who have less. These two things, earning and serving, are connected,.

I ask him what he thinks our society needs in order to be healed.

He says that we need to be more aware of values. Reign in our selfishness. Where individual interests dominate, the common good loses. Selfishness is just thinking of your own advantage without any consideration for anyone around you. We are selfish if we take more than our share. Here is an example: we put a dent in our car and take it to the shop. The mechanic says, "Well, I'll also do the rusty fender while I'm at it." That is taking more than our share. The attitude of entitlement, of looking out to get what we think we deserve with utter disregard for others is a big problem in our society.

And, I might add, in our companies. We really need to rethink that attitude!

"Please, Ms. Wittmann, that's a naïve illusion," some will say. And I do often wonder whether it is illusion or reality. Strictly speaking, I have been wondering about that since I first traveled on the Native path for a while.

One thing is clear: there is never going to be a moment in which *all* employees in a company will be on the same level of development. But for me, it is essential that at least the members of the leadership team have a healthy ego and take out their "personal trash" on a regular basis.

When they do, astonishing things will happen, such as:

- The manager leads by example and becomes a role model for her team.
- The manager has much more power and energy, feels more balanced, and becomes more resistant to turbulence.
- The manager makes clear decisions and can communicate and explain them.
- The manager does not lose energy in unnecessary fights, e.g., personal conflicts, and can use all of her energy to lead the team.
- The manager is less disappointed, angry, and frustrated. Sure, there are moments when she feels the pinch, but she

is always able to look forward again and keep an eye on the big picture.

And another very important point: the manager is able to break away from the constant struggle to get more faster. This is the subject of my conversation with brand consultant Jon Christoph Berndt, an expert on human branding. Many people think that branding is first of all about packaging, about design, price points, and appearances. But a brand is much more; it is the roof under which a company can develop its personality. And people can discover theirs.

"People need to listen to their inner voices again and dare to follow the things that make them happy and content." In this statement, Jon Christoph Berndt doesn't mean that we all need to camp out in the forest in teepees; he means that we need to explore our own source of spiritual and emotional wealth. In his opinion, part of that process is not doing everything in the race of life, not taking every offer, even if it is "on trend": Facebook, social media … just out of fear that we won't be there on the *one* night when we would get the business card of our life.

Yes, he likes nice things. He likes to fly to New York City and Barcelona. But in Germany, he rides trains and uses a car-sharing model—not because he cannot afford a car. He is authentic, I realize, more than many other people I know. He is aware that there are some people in his company who know more about certain things than he does. And he is grateful when those colleagues handle a customer's project that needs their expertise. Letting go, without resentment, without a bruised ego—it takes effort to get to this point.

However, he does say that there is no perfect authenticity. In his own life, he tries to get closer to his own authenticity. For him, this means discovering that a country hotel on Lake Starnberg for eighty dollars per night is good enough when he is working on a new book; it doesn't have to be the New York City designer hotel for $350. Ask yourself: What do I really need to be happy and content?

And it also needs to be possible that he, as a leader, is able to go to a staff meeting on Monday morning and say, "Guys, my father is dying. Please bear with me this week." Even a few years ago, it would have been unthinkable to many people in leadership positions to show emotions and make themselves vulnerable. This is also part of a healthy ego.

And another thing is just as important for leaders as for brands: strong brands polarize. Not everybody likes them. But strong brands take a position and show where they stand.

If a leader is a brand, we will have lots of fans on the one hand and detractors on the other. But we need this strong inner position to be a chief. Then we can be vulnerable every once in a while without losing face.

But back to the question of illusion or reality.

Of course a university degree and job experience is not enough to bring out a person's whole personality and make them authentic. To support the personal development of leaders, we need additional programs. When the leaders are "grown up," their teams have room for their personal and professional development.

Unfolding your personality, growing as a person, is a lifelong process. It doesn't happen overnight. It takes a lot of courage to face your own inner construction sites, start building things, and maybe realize along the way that someone else is better suited for your own position.

At the same time, life doesn't leave us out in the rain. If somebody else fits our spot better than we do, it only means that there is something better out there for us! Fortune favors the brave! What are we waiting for?

For small companies in particular, this kind of personal development means a clear competitive edge, because they can act quickly. Big corporate groups need some time to implement the concept group-wide. But even individual teams can move a lot. And little strokes fell big oaks.

Something for your medicine bag: Off the top of your head, what is your symbol for a "healthy ego"? Put it in your medicine bag. Which situations tend to throw you off-balance? Make notes on the situation, its trigger, and possible new ways of handling it.

Results of your medicine walk, with the subject "Healthy Ego and Sense of Self":

CHAPTER 5

Responsibility for Everything That Happens (or Doesn't)

One day, during a very cold winter that lasted for a long time, a young warrior got into a fight with his twin brother, Daring Crow, who was only a few minutes older but felt superior to his brother in many ways. Daring Crow read the buffalo tracks very differently from his brother, who had been made the leader of the hunt for the first time. The tribe's meat reserves were almost gone, so the decision of which tracks to follow was of great consequence. If they were to come back without their quarry, their tribe would have to go hungry, which was dangerous, especially for newborns and their nursing mothers. Which way to go?

The brothers fought so long and passionately and brought up so many old conflicts that they didn't notice the sky darkening. There was a snowstorm lasting several hours. The two warriors waited out the storm in an abandoned bear cave. When the sky cleared at last, the few buffalo tracks the brothers had fought over were hidden by a thick blanket of snow. Daring Crow was very angry, and his younger brother decided to follow his suggestion. Together, they took the path Daring Crow pointed out. But the buffalo were gone.

Without their quarry, the brothers went back to camp that night. When the chief asked about the reason, Daring Crow blamed his brother right away. His brother remained silent, even though he desperately wanted to defend himself. Finally, he said to the chief, who was looking at them both inquisitively, "I am responsible for losing the buffalo tracks."

The Chief paused and then asked the people sitting at the conference table, "What do you think, which one of the two became chief?"

Julia, the young woman, raised her hand. "You!"

* * *

If our ego is healthy, we are willing to stand by our thoughts and actions. Even if there are many other people involved. There are always other people. Even if we would have done everything differently, if we had been the only ones to decide. We would always do that. Even if it is absolutely not our fault that things happened the way they did. That is not the point. If we call ourselves a leader, we are responsible. Simple as that.

Where, in our job, does this become clear? It emerges whenever we do not reach our goals, whenever quarterly figures or project deadlines are not met. People are usually quick to point fingers, to find fault with others, not with themselves. If heads will roll, let it not be ours.

Sometimes, I get the feeling that our construct of layers upon layers of hierarchies is designed to always have someone else to blame, always someone below us on the ladder to throw out—as long as our position is not undermined.

A Native American tribe has a very flat hierarchy: chief—shaman or medicine woman—the tribe. The one who keeps everything together also has to take the responsibility. There is no finger-pointing.

A chief always assumes responsibility for everything that happens. And for everything that doesn't.

I am meeting Semiha Sander, head of finance and administration at the Institute for Transformation in Business and Society (INIT). The Institute is part of the Department for Strategy, Organization & Leadership at the EBS Universität für Wirtschaft und Recht in the Rheingau region. In this position, one of her responsibilities is to make sure that the funds provided to the Institute are spent as agreed—and that everybody feels comfortable in the workplace.

On the subject of responsibility, she has been on an interesting journey: before she joined EBS, Semiha worked as an accounting and controlling manager. The company was sold to a US group. Among many other changes, she was suddenly faced with a list with names of people she needed to let go, in some cases without giving reasons. She remembers a conversation with a colleague, a mother of four, who had been with the company for a long time.

"Back then, I thought, don't show any emotions in this conversation," she says. She was not allowed to tell the woman about the list she had to "implement." The result: the colleague held Semiha Sander personally responsible for her termination and accused her of not having advocated on her behalf. At that moment, the company that had given Semiha Sander a lot over the years was dead to her. She tried to protect other colleagues and stay as long as she could—but her own health soon gave her a clear indication that it was time to go. Most people of the leadership team left the company voluntarily.

Communication, says Semiha Sander, is one of the essential components of leadership. If the executive board hides on the thirtieth floor or the boss just flies in once a month from the United States—as was the case at that company—to talk with a few managers behind closed doors without making himself available to the rest of the team, people are going to begin to ask: What am I doing here?

Due to the nature of the transaction, the sale of the company was communicated very late. But the employees need to feel that they can trust their colleagues and leaders at any time.

Semiha Sander took some time to find the path she is following today, the one that suits her personal talents and needs as a mother of two. She learned a lot and went on a journey that only few people would undertake with so much courage.

"When the former owners of the company heard what happened to the employees following the acquisition, they were shocked. If they had known what would happen to the company, they would have realized the acquisition with other partners," she says. At this point, we might ask: How far does our responsibility go?

* * *

Even a man like Claus Hipp admits that he made mistakes. In hindsight, there were things he could have done better. One thing he discovered in difficult situations was his faith. He says that there will always be difficult situations. But if you strive to act in accordance with your values, you have a clean conscience, which strengthens your position.

I fully agree with this. And for me, it begins with selecting customers. My team defines which values are important to us—in our own work environment and in our relationships with our customers. We select our customers according to these criteria and reject quick wins, which promise short-term profit but would be contrary to our culture.

On our website www.dieerstegeige.de, you will find the following under "Philosophy":

> What We Believe in and What We Stand For
>
> *Our goal is to harmonize the interactions between people and systems. In an orchestra, the first violin is the bridge between the conductor and orchestra. It brings the composer's vision to life and breathes soul into the interplay. We successfully translate this motto into IT projects.*
>
> *All employees—both yours and ours—are integrated into a project in a way that allows them to bring their individual experience and authenticity to the table. Great IT solutions don't just come from know-how; they result from a team in which every member has the chance to participate and thrive. Our IT solutions are based on this experience.*

We are convinced that your system can do more than you think—and so can you! This is what we want to develop and implement together with you at the IT level—and we want to make sure that in no time, you won't need us anymore! Once we have made ourselves superfluous, our goal is achieved.

This might sound arrogant or foolish to some people. For me as a CEO, responsible for myself, my team, our customers, and the projects, it means standing for the things that are important to us. As a chief, I have to advocate these principles—consistently and without exception—and apply them in the selection of new customers and employees.

The Internet is chock-full of websites on which companies present their values, philosophies, and visions. Are they really put into practice in everyday life? Doubtful in most cases.

* * *

Prof. Dr. Christian Berg is an interesting man. He is presidium member of the German Association for the Club of Rome, holds an honorary chair for sustainability and global change at TU Clausthal and is a frequent visiting professor of Corporate Sustainability at the Universität des Saarlandes, UdS. He has a degree in physics, studied theology and philosophy, and wrote his doctoral thesis in engineering about sustainability and networking processes.

Engineer and theologian? At first glance, this combination seems like fire and water—or Native Americans and IT. It leads him to the important questions: What keeps the world together at its core? And how should we assume stewardship of creation?

In the course of his studies, he learned about sustainability—a word people often use without really knowing the vast subject behind it.

"The challenges of sustainability," says Christian Berg, "are huge, because they transcend the boundaries of disciplines, countries, regions, industries, and political spheres." All kinds of boundaries. We all talk about interdisciplinarity, but most of the misunderstanding or ignorance of the subject comes from not really speaking the same language. "We need to learn to relate to each other, to listen and understand the situation of the other person," he says. It is helpful to know the other fields, to identify with them and to build bridges. Christian Berg is aided by his own bridge between theology and science.

Sustainability, he says, needs a new framework that doesn't exist yet: an eco-social market economy. The German model of the social state and social market economy could be used as a guiding principle but should be expanded to include environmental concerns and a global perspective.

The biggest enemy of sustainability, says Berg, is short-term thinking. We are facing strong international competition and need to find our niche by offering very attractive products, low prices, good quality—or all of them combined. Speed is a great advantage here. But right now, it makes us externalize costs. It is not easy to find the balance between short-term survival—the profitability of a company that needs to be secured as the foundation of everything else—and long-term sustainability. This is our task.

The German Association for the Club of Rome supports three initiatives that are each sustainable in their own way. There is the Club of Rome School Project for integrated, sustainable education concepts. The ThinkTank30 seeks new societal impulses by supporting the younger generation of thinkers. And there is Plant-for-the-Planet, initiated by Felix Finkbeiner. When he was nine years old, Felix Finkbeiner was supposed to give a school presentation on the subject of climate change. The question "Why aren't we doing much? Why is it so difficult for adults to get anywhere with this issue?" moved him so much that he and his father founded Plant-for-the-Planet, a global foundation with a mandate from the UN Environment Programme (UNEP).

These examples show that big changes do not happen overnight. Great things are changed in small, persistent steps. Commitment, dedication, and passion have the power to create different conditions and a different mindset that ultimately leads to changes in behavior. And to more responsibility. And our greatest chance is to be a leader who can inspire and motivate others.

From 2011 to 2012, Christian Berg headed the Sustainable Economy and Growth task force, part of Chancellor Angela Merkel's Expert Dialogue project. For about a year, six task forces worked on finding answers to the questions: How do we want to live together? By what means should we live? How do we want to learn?

Angela Merkel and the experts on the task forces invested a lot of time and energy to answer these questions. They even engaged directly with citizens in three major German cities, whose ideas were heard, selected, and discussed in a personal conversation with the chancellor.

Something for your medicine bag: Which symbol signifies responsibility for you? What helps you be aware of your responsibility for your thoughts and actions, every day and in all situations and relationships? Which values are represented on your website and need real integration in your business life and corporate culture?

Results of your medicine walk, with the subject "My Responsibility":

CHAPTER 6

Peacemaker: The Art of Waging War and Making Peace

The Chief brings a big pipe to the meeting. It is his turn to speak. By now, nobody is checking their texts and e-mails when he speaks. The Chief calmly assembles the two parts of the pipe and begins to stuff it while he tells his story.

"In our tribes, there is a man we call the pipe carrier. Carrying the pipe is one of the highest honors the tribe bestows. The one who carries the pipe has come a long way. Being pipe carrier is not a job or position; it is a way of life. The pipe carrier is committed to serving the community. He is the keeper of the sacred ceremony. In your world, you could compare him to a minister, priest, or rabbi. Indians believe that peace has several dimensions. Here in the Western world, many people believe that peace means that there is no war.

For Native Americans, peace is not the absence of war. It is the way we think, speak, and act. Peace comes from within us, not from the outside. Peace is the balance between male and female, learning and teaching, humility and pride. It is a life in harmony with everything we are and everything that surrounds us."

The Chief lights the pipe and takes a deep puff of the pipe. Then he passes it to the head of department, who thinks, *Dear God, the fire alarm.* But a look from The Chief tells him that he had better take a puff.

* * *

We don't need to watch the news on television if we want to see war. Every day, the real battles are fought in our companies. At the top of the list: power struggles. People fight to "get" more power and prestige. To climb the corporate ladder faster than the others. Add to that hurt feelings and bruised egos when people are e.g. excluded in a decision-making process. There is disappointment, anger, and frustration if others make more money or get the promotion. Then there is the fight for recognition and visibility—not to mention all the little skirmishes when people push our buttons, when we feel helpless, disenfranchised, powerless, and vulnerable.

Instead of fighting these battles out in the open, defining them and ending them one day, we remain silent. But silence doesn't bury the hatchet—it merely waits underneath the surface for the day when it is brought to light again, probably at the wrong moment.

If there were a unit of measurement for peace, Native Americans would define it as the capacity to walk this earth with an open heart, calm and unafraid.

A famous image is of the pebble that creates many ripples when it is thrown in the pond. It is the reflection of our responsibility for everything we are sending out, positive and negative. When we are at peace with ourselves, we radiate peace. If we are at odds with ourselves, we reflect that, too. We always influence the whole.

If there is a conflict in the tribe, the pipe carrier is called. He conducts the peace ceremony, in which everything has a specific meaning. In a ritual, he connects the two pieces of the pipe: male and female. It signifies that there are no differences between the participants. Everybody sees eye to eye.

With every clump of tobacco stuffed into the pipe, the participants reflect on their connection with each other and on the history of that connection. Stuffing the pipe honors all the positive aspects of this connection; it shows gratitude and visualizes the things that keep these people together.

In lighting the tobacco, the threads of this connection are woven once again. With every puff of the pipe, a new connection is created between the participants. This forms the basis for a conversation that acknowledges and honors the past, present, and future. There is no right or wrong in this round.

When the pipe carrier is called and the pipe is shared, there are certain rules that apply once the pipe is lit: everything that is said and all agreements are based in honesty and mutual understanding. The foundation is always gratitude for being able to have this moment and heal this conflict together—as a group and as individuals. Each person who takes a puff of the pipe takes a moment for self-reflection as well. Only when people are in balance can they make lasting peace.

The pipe is passed around until the tobacco is gone.

What if we had a pipe carrier in our companies? What if we had an arbiter or mediator who could be called in to moderate talks if the situation escalates?

These talks follow a certain structure given by the mediator and have to adhere to a few simple topics rules:

- Appreciation
- Gratitude
- Reflection on the personalities of the participants
- Recognition of previous successful joint effort and possible future successes
- Emphasizing the strengths of all participants
- Creating an image of peaceful cooperation

Peace is safeguarded by small, everyday things that create a culture of appreciation: honest feedback among colleagues. Gratitude for good, constructive teamwork. A few words of praise.

Sometimes you have to look a little more closely to find something praiseworthy. But it is worth the effort! Basically, we all want to be loved. Not just in our personal relationships, but at the office as well. After all, we spend a lot of time there to be able to afford what we call our "lifestyle."

Something for your medicine bag: If you were a pipe carrier, which conversation is urgently necessary? Between which parties? How would you go about that? What would be the best goal? How could all parties appreciate each other and come to an agreement? Place a little tobacco in your medicine bag. And play the pipe carrier every once in a while—in your thoughts or at the office. Offer to serve as a moderator, even if nobody has ever asked you to do it!

Results of your medicine walk, with the subject "Making Peace":

CHAPTER 7

Wisdom: The Leadership Potential of a Mature Soul

It is 10:00 a.m. Time for a coffee break. Interestingly, since The Chief has joined the company, the breaks have stopped being gossip sessions around the coffeemaker. People talk to each other in a different way. Bitching about the boss or absent colleagues has been reduced to a minimum. Instead, people are focusing on topics relevant to the team's work on current tasks. The vocabulary of the team members has expanded as well, to include words never spoken before in this office. One of those words is *maturity*. While the cappuccino is percolating, someone from Accounting asks The Chief what it means to have a mature soul.

The Chief answers, "The sun is scorching the prairie without mercy. The grass is dry. There hasn't been any rain for weeks. With their soft lips, the horses pluck the meager stalks from the cracked earth. Among them is a black stallion, whose coat reflects the sunlight as if it was made from polished leather. Today is a big day for Red Eagle, a young warrior. Today, he will receive his own horse. This beautiful black stallion is meant for him. Getting a horse is the first step to becoming a man, the first step on the long path to becoming a warrior. If Red Eagle can prove that he is able to be responsible for another creature, he will be allowed to go with the hunting party one day. He will wear their moccasins, observe them, and learn. He will learn to take responsibility for many and think on his feet. In time, he will be given more responsibility until he will lead the hunt one day and coordinate the hunters. Then, his job will be to make sure that no warrior or horse is lost on the hunt. Once he manages to lead his hunting party, he has taken the step from boy to man, the next step on his path toward a mature soul."

Everybody has listened intently to The Chief. None of the colleagues even took a sip from their mugs.

* * *

The transition from one phase of life to the next, from boy to man or from girl to woman, is one of the Indian rites of passage. Of course, young girls have their transitions and rituals that mark their emergence as an adult. The first important step toward maturity in a woman's life is her first menstrual cycle. She is initiated into the community of women, who welcome her feminine power. This is a big day for the tribe, because every woman is a "creator of the world." Women have an important status in the tribe, because they carry the cycle of life and death. When a woman's cycle awakens, she brings her creativity, femininity, and the continuation of the ancestral line to the tribe.

In the tribe, young and old people live and work closely together. Indians say that this is the only way to gain wisdom. The entire village and, most importantly, the elders participate in all rites of passage. They watch, support, and confirm the adolescents and reward them for working on their own person and for the good of the community.

Which Phases of Life and Growth Do We Know in Our World?

We recognize certain phases in our personal lives: birth, childhood, adulthood, death.

But we also go through important phases in our processional life, which we rarely acknowledge or even recognize: high school diploma, college, career start, leadership roles, retirement.

What happens when a person reaches a new phase by being promoted, for example? He gets new business cards, and his pay stubs and tax return show different numbers. This is promotion on paper. Nothing more!

When does a manager truly become a manager? Which steps did he take on his path to becoming a warrior? Where did he prove that he worked on his own person and for the good of the community?

This development has become a part of everyday life in many companies—and it fills me with concern. Actually, I think it is rather negligent toward the employees and the new manager.

A summa-cum degree does not make a manager. Gaining wisdom and the ability to make good decisions is a process that takes years. And it needs a path with steps toward maturity, which must be clearly visible—and should be celebrated!

Wisdom cannot be learned. Wisdom must be earned. Knowledge and wisdom are related, but while knowledge is transitory and is constantly rendered obsolete by new knowledge, wisdom is the one that remains. Even if we were to sum up all our knowledge, it would not amount to wisdom!

Wisdom has a lot to do with emotional intelligence, with life experience and intuition. It means embracing life with all its facets and with all our talents and weaknesses. It is the daily look in the mirror of our thoughts, emotions, and actions.

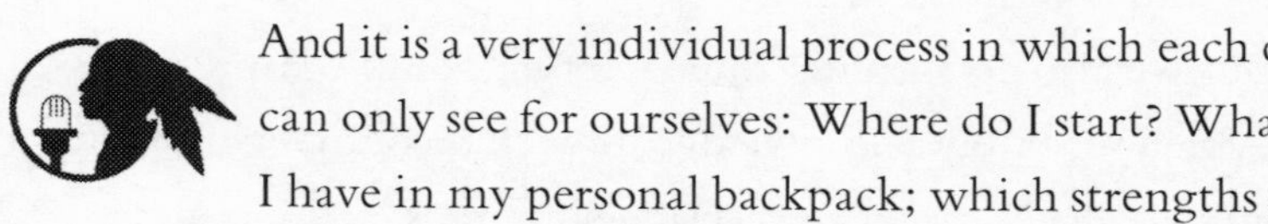

And it is a very individual process in which each of us can only see for ourselves: Where do I start? What do I have in my personal backpack; which strengths give me wings and which things weigh me down? This takes time. And a certain amount of patience. No two employees are alike in this process. *Time* and *patience* are two keywords Theo Knaus mentioned in our conversation. "Companies need to give their employees the chance to follow their path, to gain experience and learn from it. They need to be able to bear the responsibility for their own mistakes."

The Hopi say that wisdom comes to us only when we stop looking for it. When we begin to live the life our Creator has conceived for us. And wisdom is not connected to age. We all know young wise people and old fools.

> "Seek wisdom, not knowledge. Knowledge is of the past. Wisdom is of the future."
>
> –Lumbee proverb

The Swiss education reformer Heinrich Pestalozzi called for the triad of "mind, skill, and spirit." Claus Hipp mentions Pestalozzi when he talks about the trainee programs for his new hires. In his company, the young people are not just taught facts and figures of the business. In the age of electronic knowledge storage, it is important to him not to weigh down their minds. Instead, he wants to focus on creativity. He likes young people who find solutions. Claus Hipp found an outlet for his creativity in his paintings—and he is known for taking his young employees to the opera, on occasion.

How long will he continue to share his wisdom with the company? "I am going to work as long as my children think they need me," he says. "My kids are honest enough to tell me when I am no longer fit enough to do this."

Something for your medicine bag: What symbolizes wisdom to you? What are the phases you have gone through in your life and your career; which thresholds did you pass? And which of them gave you the deepest insights? Which would you celebrate? And which phases are still ahead of you? How will you be able to master them? What do you need—and who will support you?

Results of your medicine walk, with the subject "My Wisdom":

CHAPTER 8

Growing Roots: Feeling at Home as a Business Nomad

An outdoor meeting? Really? Yes, really. The Chief called the meeting. Well, then. Still—sitting in the grass, like kindergarteners, in your custom suit? It's a challenge.

The Chief passes a staff around, festooned with leather strips and three beautiful feathers. It is a talking staff. The person who holds it speaks. All others keep their mouths shut. It's that simple. Every person is asked to tell the others where they are from, where their home is. Is that relevant to the project? They all have so much to do. Tulsa, we hear. San Francisco. Dallas. Atlanta. Des Moines. Rapid City. Hartford. Tallahassee. Ann Arbor. Mobile. Terre Haute … if you were to find the cities the team is naming on a map and draw lines to connect them, the result would be a grid crisscrossing the country. So many different places. So many people with different dispositions and homes.

"Indians call trees 'standing people,'" says The Chief when the talking staff reaches him, after he names a small town north of Tucson, Arizona, as his home. "Trees and people have roots reaching deep and far back. A tree trunk is like the human spine. Its branches are arms," explains The Chief. "The Seneca say that all trees have more roots than branches."

Julia, the young woman, glances respectfully at the group of trees not far from their meeting place. The sun is breaking through the treetops. As tall as those trees are, they must be at least a hundred years old, much older than the company they are working for. Julia imagines how deep and strong their roots must be, if they are a hundred years old, and how they reach out in the ground, unseen by the human eye, to connect this small group of people sitting in a circle—each with roots in the soil of a different home.

* * *

What are our roots? When and where do we grow them to feel grounded, especially in this day and age, when we wander from one place to the next, one job to the next?

Home is more than a place. It is a sense of belonging. The word *longing* is in there, because we long for something. In order to know where my place is, I need to know what I am longing for.

And I need to know what my values and traditions are. A tree always remains in its place, rooted to the ground, being nourished by the soil—while nourishing its surroundings at the same time. Humans, on the other hand, are always on the move. Some Native Americans say that trees can be our greatest teachers. By considering these quiet giants, we can learn to stand tall in our life. The roots run underneath the surface; most of them are invisible. But they show themselves in a storm, when the tree can resist the strong winds and remain standing. With deep roots, you are able to embrace life and move with its rhythm. The first gusts of wind in life, events that occur in people's professional lives for example, quickly show who will stumble and fall and who is able to move *with* the events.

Unlike trees, we can be aware of our roots. Knowing our roots means knowing what nourishes our body, mind, and spirit. We can walk tall. We have found our balance. We are tapping into the natural source of our strength. And we understand the circle of giving and taking, which enables us to be at home all over the world.

As a manager and leader, we need to confront our teams constantly with the present and future of the company—but we also need to let them feel their roots, so that they can be part of a project as a person with a history and with all the insights gained in the course of their lives.

What Are Our Roots?

- our values and convictions
- our visions and dreams
- our ancestors and our background
- our talents and our potential

Indians would even say that without knowing our roots, we are unable to live to our potential or realize our dreams and visions. This is not just true for the chief, but for the entire tribe.

Just like the roots of a plant, our roots need to be watered and treated with care. Some roots wither and die over the years; some grow deeper. And sometimes, new roots grow. It is a structure that changes constantly and needs to be revisited from time to time.

What Can We Do to Feel Our Roots and Keep Ourselves Grounded?

We need to take time for ourselves, as individuals or as a team—perhaps with a day spent outdoors or in a place that gives us strength. When we take time to spend by ourselves or with our team, we feel and see our roots. If we don't do it, we become uprooted over time, as a person and as a company. That makes it difficult for us to hold our ground in life and on the market and almost impossible to stand for clear positions. Without a firm stand, there is no clear direction. And if the direction is missing, there cannot be trust and confidence—our own or the trust and confidence of others. It is a cycle, a wheel that always goes back to our roots.

How Can We Feel at Home in a World in Which Many People Move on to a New Job or Country Every Few Years?

As I said before, a person's home is not a specific place or building, but comes with a sense of belonging, community, and friendship. *Community* is a generous term. It can be your family, the team at the office, or your church. A community is a group of people who share the same beliefs, dreams, and visions.

Often, we become uprooted when we lose our sense of true community. Social networks can help, but only to a certain point. True friendships happen on a deeper level and survive geographic separation. We can take them with us and stretch them around the entire globe.

For many Indians, home was the place where they happened to be, because the entire tribe moved to a new place. To them, it was perfectly natural to grow roots in any new place.

Today, we experience many moves to new places, so there are a few important things all leaders and employees must keep in mind:

- We need to know and nourish our roots, because they help us to take a firm stand in the new place.
- We need to maintain relationships with our loved ones—beyond Facebook and Twitter.
- We need to find and integrate into a new tribe—clubs, churches, teams of any kind, just as long as we find people who share our interests.
- We need to stay in touch with nature—in the city and, more importantly, outside of it, where nature surrounds us.

Where Is the Best Home for a Company?

Ideally, a company should offer a sense of belonging, too. We want to belong to something. A physical place where all employees feel good and welcome is important, but it doesn't have to be overemphasized. You can cultivate a sense of community anywhere. It is not about the appearance or expensive furniture in this place but about taking time to be with each other instead of rushing at record speed through a huge palace of glass and steel.

Another aspect is often overlooked in today's world: all companies and all entrepreneurs have a social responsibility. Often, entire companies are hastily moved to a new location, to a new city that offers the best incentives and subsidies. And just as hastily, the locations are abandoned again. If you open a business in a place, you take on responsibility for the place.

Globality comes with a price. It gives us opportunities all over the world, but it also challenges us to stay in touch, to be curious about others and ourselves—and to take some time to have a good, old-fashioned cup of coffee face-to-face.

Globality also challenges us to be alert and honest with ourselves. Our international business operations are the jewel in our crown. But how much can we really handle? What makes sense on a global scale? I keep thinking about one thing Theo Knaus said in our conversation: "When a company wants to go global, many things need to be considered. Even the top-tier leadership team of the group often lacks the ability to see the entire sphere of influence. They focus on profit and shareholder values, because these things are generally acceptable concerns for which they will get accolades. Looking more closely, you will see that companies turning huge profits often have one or several areas where someone or something suffers. People. Or nature. Because we have not fully understood and internalized the entire system with all its facets and complexities."

The Teaching of the Shawl

For Native Americans, the concept of home changed when they were forced to live on reservations and integrate into the world of white people. Home, which had been marked by human relationships, being connected with nature, and preserving traditions, now had to fit into four walls. Many Indians were unable to keep their traditions; some turned away from them. A few tried to go back to their roots and live in their old homelands, where their hearts lived. They accepted the consequence of having to live in their traditional dwellings that were less comfortable than the houses on the reservations (though few of those were more than shacks). Still, those dwellings gave them back a sense of home. Each person who decided to leave the world of white people and return to nature and the elders received a shawl as a symbol for nature embracing every person returning home.

After this step, once the decision was made, the person returning had to ask permission to re-enter the world of tradition.

The metaphor of the shawl is still valid in today's world. The shawl reminds us that true progress can only be achieved if we work with others. It tells us that it is important to remember where we come from and the people who stand for the things that are important to us. It asks us to share our experiences and let other people into our lives, as we are a part of theirs.

In times of separation, the shawl can also be a symbol for a warm embrace and a sign that this connection will last forever. It is our decision whether we want to commit to such deep connections—just like the Native Americans who decide to go back to the place that warms their heart.

Something for your medicine bag: The more we, as leaders, are aware of our roots, the better we can weather the conflicts and storms of life. Pause for a moment. Where do you come from? What is your origin; who are your ancestors? What is their story? What symbol stands for you and your roots that give you the strength to survive today, tomorrow, and the day after? Could this year's Christmas present to your employees be a shawl, a sign of the connectedness between different people, homelands, stories, and potentials coming together to achieve a great goal?

Results of your medicine walk, with the subject "My Roots":

____

____

____

____

____

____

____

____

CHAPTER 9

Who Is the Strong Woman at the Chief's Side?

"Why are there not more women here?" The Chief asks one day in a meeting.

The question is met with silence and coughing.

Nobody dares to mention that this company is not exactly an illustration of practical affirmative action.

"Without women, the tribe dies," The Chief says. He gets up and leaves the room.

* * *

Many Native American tribes had clear roles for men and women. Women were often responsible for

- loyalty;
- compassion;
- hospitality;
- sense of community;

- sharing; and
- selflessness in balance with self-care.

Women were revered as the creative forces who gave life at all levels. They were entrusted with the important task of caring for everybody—for the children, for the leaders, for the weak and the warriors. But their most important responsibility was to care for people's dreams.

Women had a high status in the tribe, because they followed the path of beauty. They recognize beauty in themselves, in their surroundings, and in others. And they teach others to recognize their own beauty.

In the tribe, women and men were equally recognized for their talents and commitment. There was no power struggle, because both roles were equally important and secured survival. Women were women. And men were men. Period.

Today, some women feel pushed into or reduced to a certain role. In trying to avoid that, they try to emulate men—more or less successfully.

What would happen if we women were to combine our efforts to fulfill our dreams with our true talents instead of copying men? What if we were to think outside of the box and explore the chances and liberties of our role instead of its limits?

Interestingly, women having their period—they are said to experience their "moon time"— In Native American cultures, women having their period are relieved of their tasks. Moon time is a sacred time symbolizing a woman's connection with life and death. If this sacred break were taken away, it would threaten the survival and growth of the tribe. Women would use this time to reaffirm their faith in the cycle. In some tribes, women were the mediators in case of conflict and important questions. They had the final word, so it was important to cultivate their powers on a regular basis.

Something special for a woman's medicine bag: What could symbolize your cycle, your connectedness with the eternal cycle of becoming and passing? During moon time, how could you take a break to reflect and recharge your feminine energy?

Results of your medicine walk, with the subject "Female Power":

CHAPTER 10

Who Coaches the Chief? The Importance of Medicine Men and Women

The Chief knocks in the door of the HR department and enters. "I would like to see the medicine man," he says.

"We don't have a medicine man," replies the HR manager, who has gotten used to a lot of weird things in recent weeks and months. He has no trouble saying words like *medicine man* or *mature soul.* Actually, he finds himself looking for mature souls among the applicants in the latest interviews.

"You don't have a medicine man?" The Chief asks incredulously.

"Well, we have an executive board and employee representatives," the HR manager answers.

"Can they make rain and connect to the Great Spirit?" asks The Chief.

No, they can't make rain. But they can *make a fuss*, the HR manager thinks.

"When you say Great Spirit, do you mean our CEO? Would you like to make an appointment with him? That is going to take a while," he says, so The Chief won't have false hopes.

"I need the man or woman responsible for the soul of the company," says The Chief.

"I see." The HR manager clicks through his database. Product Development, Controlling, Procurement, Sales, Marketing, Accounting … but who on earth is the soul of the company?

*   *   *

While the chief leads the tribe, the medicine man is said to have the gift of inspiration and healing. Medicine men were able to connect to the spirit world. They laid hands on sick people, prayed, sang, and had many other powerful healing methods.

Medicine men were revered tribe members. Yet, medicine women were even more revered. Many Native Americans believed that women had even more healing powers. Some tribes had both a medicine man and woman, while some had just one.

Medicine men and women usually lived outside of the tribal community in order to focus entirely on their skills. It helped them keep their distance from everyday life, and they served as advisors in cases of conflict. Their tents were painted differently than the rest, as a sign for all who needed help. In some tribes, medicine women refrained from having a family and children in order to dedicate themselves to their work.

Medicine men and women were the midwives of the soul and the link to the soul of everything, the Great Spirit. They were the ones with the best connections "upstairs." And they were the go-betweens for man and nature. All their lives, they were trained like nobody else in the tribe; yet, they had the smallest egos. Without a medicine man or woman, the tribe feared for its health and survival.

The knowledge of healing body, mind, and spirit was passed down through the generations of a family. If there were no children, in some cases, the knowledge was shared with people outside of the family. The man or woman committed to following this path knew that the goal would not be reached in a few sessions or with a year of training. It would require a life of learning.

Medicine men and women were called when something important was happening in the tribe that required the support of the spirits, e.g., a hunt. The medicine man then led the tribe in prayer for a good hunt.

For the chief, the medicine man and woman were important advisors and partners. They made sure that the chief found his balance again, because even a chief is just human.

Who Are the Medicine Men and Women in the Corporate World Today?

Every good leader needs a good coach who will support his growth process and reflects his progress. For Native Americans, the medicine man or woman was someone who often didn't live in the community. In a corporate environment, it is a good idea to have the coach of the leadership team come from the outside.

Not all coaches are the same. To make the points in this book, no purely systemic knowledge is necessary. A coach for managers who want to lead with wisdom and maturity is a person who needs to work on himself constantly. For some, this goes without saying and is just part of their job description. However, not everybody sees it that way. Therefore, a good coach needs to have a solid foundation of training and keep learning throughout his career. He knows that his education and certificates will only take him so far. He knows that he needs to foster his personal growth and has implemented rituals in his daily life to keep himself grounded and balanced.

And he never draws attention to himself or his methods, but instead focuses on people and their tasks.

Ute Küffner is a woman who works that way. I met her during our time at SAP. We had a problem in our team and HR sent us Ute, a professional coach. She resolved the deadlocked situation in our team with such ease that I became curious. Shortly after that, I registered for co-active coaching training, and we have become companions on our path of self-discovery. I appreciate her as a coaching colleague and for the way she always tries to bring new elements into her work to be able to go even deeper with people. With some clients, she uses elements from dance therapy or from inner-child work—whatever is right for the person.

She invites managers who work with her to look inside and see clearly their own strengths, values, visions, and fears. Understanding themselves, they are able to be authentic and inspired leaders. It is all done for the purpose of aligning their skills with the goal of creating lasting value for the company. As an external coach, Ute is neutral, which helps her with being successful.

How Do You Recognize a Good Coach?

You can ask the coach questions and get answers. These questions could be:

- What was the phase in your life that shaped you the most?
- What were your key learnings?
- What training and workshops have you completed to let your soul mature?
- How do you take care of your muse?
- What rituals help you stay balanced or find your balance?
- Where do you go for advice when you don't know what to do? (Every good coach has a coach.)
- What holds you together on the inside when everything around you is crashing down?
- Is there a credo you live by?

In the following, I am going to give you a few answers I give potential clients who want to find out whether we are a good fit for each other:

- I think the most important phase was to experience a good friend's path to death. It was shocking to be so close to mortality, but it was also an honor to be with her.
- I became painfully aware that physical death is a reality in our lives, but we can choose to spend the time we have with purpose and fulfillment.
- I visited workshops to include nature more in my work as a coach. These experiences in the wild have helped me mature a little bit each time.

- I love poetry. Rilke's *Book of Hours* is my favorite.
- I take a break at least once per quarter. Mostly, it's a long weekend, when I just read poetry, go on hikes, and just let my soul wander.
- I meditate daily to find and keep my balance. I work with a coach on a regular basis. It has become a necessity for me.
- What holds me is the belief that we have come into the world with a purpose and my love of nature.
- My creed: "Be the change you want to see in the world." (M. K. Gandhi)

Something for your medicine bag: Who could be your medicine man or woman? What would you like to work on; in which areas would you like to grow, expand, or at least meet with others on a regular basis to reflect on the status quo? Find a symbol for your growth and place it in your medicine bag. And find a coach you trust.

Results of your medicine walk, with the subject "My Development":

CHAPTER 11

Test: Could You Be a Chief?

Now you know the main characteristics and personality traits of a chief. Time to take stock: How far did you explore each area? Did you make notes of your development potential for each chapter? Did you find topics where you had a hard time finding answers? Now you have a chance to look at where you stand, how well you know yourself, and where you would like your development to go.

You can use the following graphic to write down how comfortable you are with each area or how much you have already explored in your life.

The center of the graphic has a value of zero.

The tip of the star graphic has a value of ten.

Fill in your personal current value for each ray of the star that has a dot.

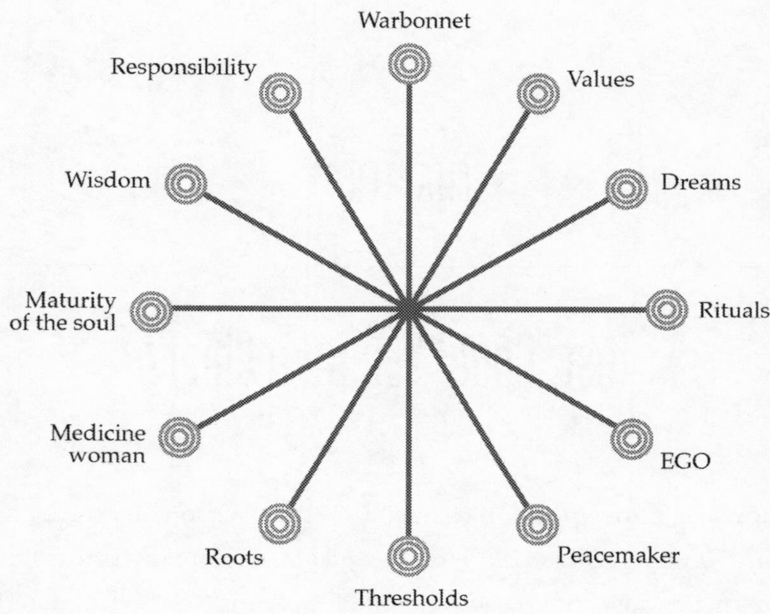

Figure 2: Could you be a Chief

Warbonnet:	The feather headdress—what are your successes?
Values:	Do you know your values? Do you know what is important to you?
Dreams:	Do you know your dream? Is your Dream Board alive with images and emotions?
Rituals:	Which personal rituals help you find your balance?
Ego:	What are triggers that make you mad?
Peacemaker:	Do you have relationships in your life that need clarification?
Thresholds:	What were the important thresholds in your life?

Roots:	What are your roots? How strong are you?
Medicine woman:	Do you have support on your way?
Maturity of the soul:	What are the next steps on your path to growth?
Wisdom:	Can you say what wisdom is for you?
Responsibility:	Do you take full responsibility for your thoughts and actions?

Done? Now connect the dots with each other. The result will be the snapshot of your current situation. Ideally, it will look like a wheel.

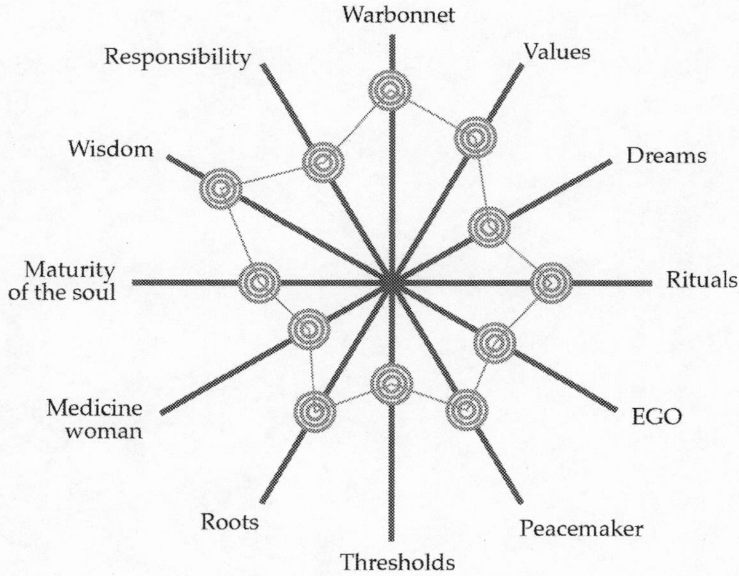

Figure 3: Could you be a Chief

Does your wheel rather look like a rickety umbrella that doesn't really open anymore? Those are the areas you should look at closely.

PART 2

The Corporate Wheel

CHAPTER 12

The Wheel of Life: Living and Working with a Natural Rhythm

It is fall. The leaves are falling. The Chief enjoys the rustling of the foliage under his moccasins as he walks to the office. The people around him seem stressed. Especially now, in the months before the winter, there is so much they still need to accomplish while planning the new year at the same time!

The Chief picks up a particularly beautiful leaf gleaming in gold and red, which has just tumbled down at his feet. It contains the power of an entire year. A child is passing him on a scooter, smiling at him. In a perfect rhythm, he pushes off several times with his right foot before embracing the joy of the ride, then pushing off again—completely at ease with himself, the path, and the wind. *Nature knows when it is time to let go and gather strength in order to come to life again with full drive and zeal at just the right moment,* thinks The Chief. He takes the leaf to the office. The meeting is going to start in five minutes.

* * *

In Indian culture, the wheel of life is sometimes called the medicine wheel. It shows the interconnectedness of all life: just as nature is moving steadily through the four seasons, unchangeable by human hands, people and even companies go through several different life cycles.

The wheel of life is a cycle of becoming and passing that can be applied to all parts of our life and work. The goal is to create balance, harmony, and health—in all areas, for the individual and the entire community.

The center of the wheel has special meaning: Native Americans say that it represents the fire of the children. It is supposed to remind us that all the things we decide to create are for our children, for the next seven generations. Therefore, all decisions should be made thoughtfully and with great care so that they become good, balanced decisions, honoring the people who came before us and including the people who will come after us.

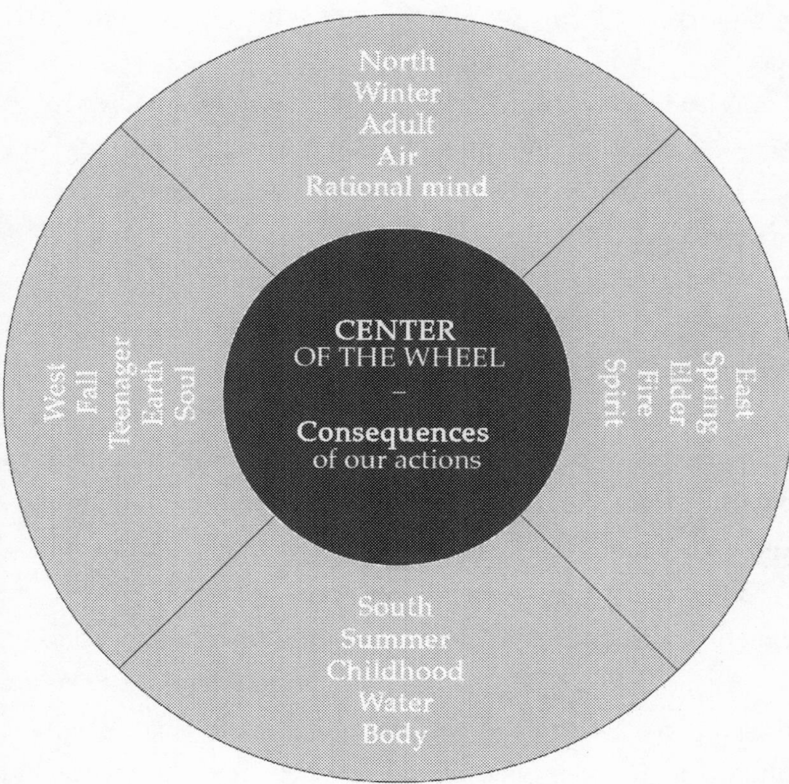

Figure 4: The wheel of life: The four segments, called shields, represent all aspects of human beings that are in or out of balance and out of it.

People go through the cycles of growth as well; they are called childhood, adolescence, adulthood, and old age.

While a child is still living with carefree spontaneity, in the flow, curious, with unbridled feelings, living every day as pure adventure, we begin to ask questions when we are teenagers, such as:

What is beauty? Am I beautiful? What is right; what is wrong? Did I do that right? Where do I belong; where is my tribe? Do I want to be different from the others? Who says what? What are my talents?

We are looking for our values, which means that we sometimes clash with those who went before us to look for their (supposed) values and found them.

Our clarity grows, until we are adults and become aware of ourselves, of our responsibility, our duty. We have defined ourselves, now mobilizing powers that we aim at our community, and we ask ourselves: What is my contribution to this world?

One day, when we reach the level of the wise elder, we experience true freedom, meaning, transformation, and soul.

All old cultures have always had transition rituals that marked the end of one stage and the beginning of the next. The most important transition seems to be that between adolescence and adulthood. The male members of a community and the girls who are becoming women are being celebrated with special ceremonies (vision quest, dances, etc.). We have already talked about this in Part 1, "The rites of passage."

For Native Americans, the wheel of life is the foundation of the past, present, and future. By understanding the wheel of life, we can remain calm and relaxed even in times of great challenges and use the power that is available to us at the time. We know that in the current phase, we can only do the things that we must do now. The homework for the next cycle will reveal itself—and make sense—once the new cycle has begun. If we embrace this rhythm, we are able to remain centered even in turbulent times.

What Does That Mean for Our Company?

Companies, teams, and products are going through a perpetual development cycle. Teams learn to function together as each individual is growing. Products and services can be developed when teams and individuals are growing.

However, every successful growth spurt begins with the chief. Only when the chief is constantly working on his inner balance, when his four shields, as the four directions and elements are called, are in balance, he can become the strong center of the corporate and tribal cycle.

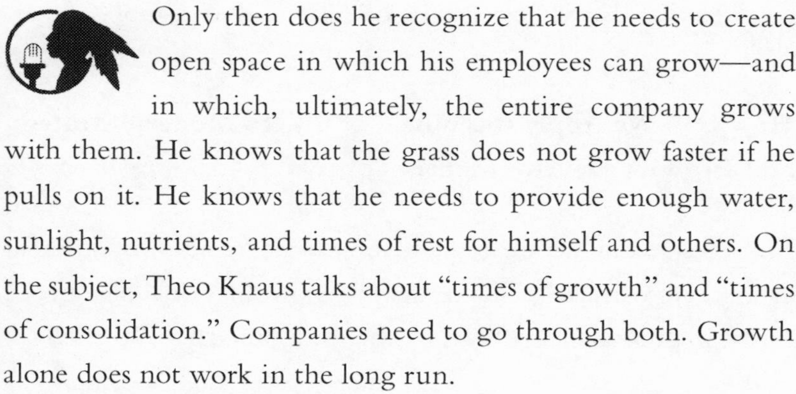

Only then does he recognize that he needs to create open space in which his employees can grow—and in which, ultimately, the entire company grows with them. He knows that the grass does not grow faster if he pulls on it. He knows that he needs to provide enough water, sunlight, nutrients, and times of rest for himself and others. On the subject, Theo Knaus talks about "times of growth" and "times of consolidation." Companies need to go through both. Growth alone does not work in the long run.

There is another interesting aspect to this: when people go through these phases, always looking for their fixed star, it makes us equal to one another. Suddenly, leadership is no longer about power but about driving the development of each individual. Then a leader can give others the space to grow. Not by taking over their growth process, but by giving them an opportunity to grow deeper roots in the earth, stretch out their branches higher into the sky, and grow more leaves—and maybe even grow some imaginative branches that might not even fit the tree at first glance. "We need some less-than-perfect trees," Theo would say. Yes!

> "This is what a good chief would want: that we take the place that suits us, that fulfills us and challenges us at the same time. I'm glad to be a member of the tribe; I follow my chief Barbara and support her whenever I can. I am very happy, I can discover my own strength without any pressure, and if it is necessary, I am ready to give 150%, because everything is just right!"
>
> –Viola Cester, DIE ERSTE GEIGE GmbH

How Can We Apply the Wheel of Life to Modern Strategy and Product Development?

In the following, we are going to look at the interplay of different cycles and wheels in the company—how they influence each other, in great and small ways, every day, 365 days of the year.

CHAPTER 13

The Corporate Wheel: Product Development in Line with Human Development

There are countless theories about optimizing innovation cycles and product life cycles. One thing is usually ignored:

Innovations are created by people, not machines. The employees and corporate culture are always shaping the products.

This means that product development is always closely connected with employee development. Every product innovation cycle impacts people—and the other way around. Every human development shapes the product. When new products are created, there are always new (and well-known) human qualities and talents coming to light. While focusing on product cycles and marketing quadrants, you cannot afford to ignore this.

The entire system is a cogwheel with an endless number of small and larger cogs and connecting pieces—all of them meshing together. I am going to reduce them to four major cycles here, which can help us understand the big picture.

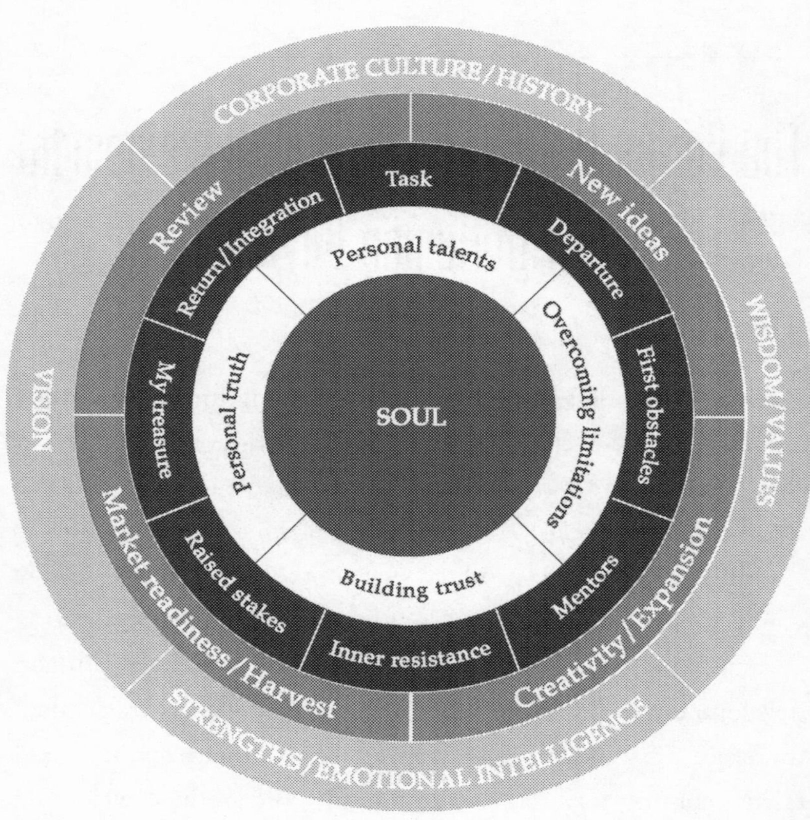

Figure 5: The corporate wheel and its four growth cycles

The corporate wheel is a moving circle. It is not static; it is not fixed or set in stone, unlike many philosophies, values, and mission statements defined in corporate meetings. They are often good and nice to read. But who ensures that the philosophies, values, and missions are being *lived*? Who sends employees and products to an annual prevention check-up to examine them for vitality and viability? Are the products still breathing? Are the employees still breathing? Are their hearts still beating for the development of new ideas? How is their lifeblood? Did we act according to our values? What could we do better? How can our corporate culture be enriched by the stories surrounding our products and employees? Does everybody still remember where it all began and where our journey is supposed to take us?

Four major cycles keep the corporate wheel going—every day, all year long, whether or not we are aware of it:

1. The cycle of the chief
2. The cycle of the employee (hero's journey)
3. The innovation cycle
4. The cycle of the company

At the center of these four cycles is the soul of the company, the corporate fire that connects all, people and products. It is what makes us unique as people and as a company and what binds us together. The soul of the company is invisible, yet ever present. Just like people have an immortal soul we cannot see, which is forever a part of us and will survive our body and mind.

The soul of the company is the foundation for product innovation and the personal development of each individual employee. The soul of the company can grow only if the chief is aware that his soul exists. Or, as Theo Knaus would say: "the soul of the company is an independent entity that grows and develops. It is connected to the company's meaningfulness, to the corporate culture that can sustain and survive. It makes sense for the entire system—not just the shareholders."

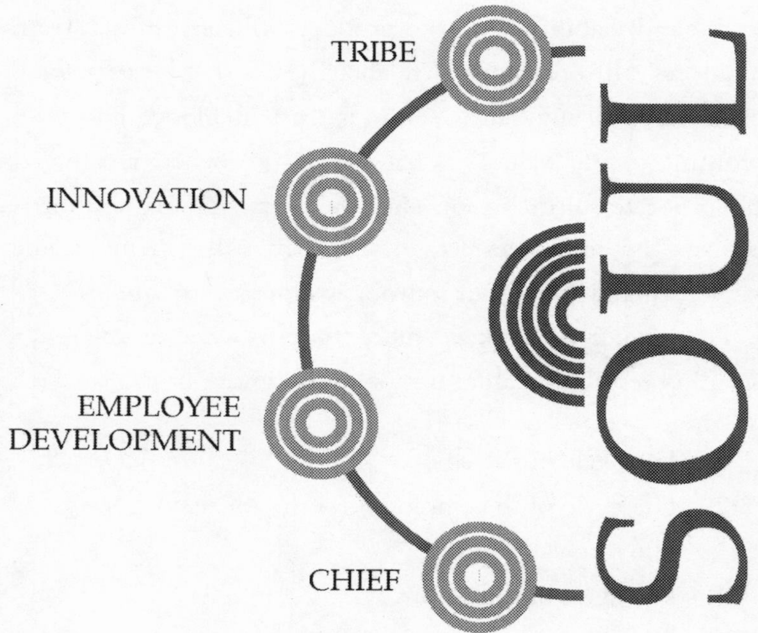

Figure 6: The corporate soul – the spine connecting the chief, employee development, innovation, and the tribe.

The First Cycle: Cycle of the Chief

As we have seen in part 1, the company and its soul live and die with the chief (in big companies: with the chiefs).

The more the chief bares his soul, the more he knows what holds him on the inside, the more he is able to recognize his talents and limitations, thus finding his own truth. Then he is able to get his employees excited about following new paths.

As so often, actions speak louder than words: the employees notice if the chief is centered and steadfast. Only then do they trust him and are willing to follow his lead to make any necessary changes. Do we follow the instructions of the pilot who doesn't know his aircraft and gets nervous with the smallest turbulence?

Recalling my own experiences of the past few years, I can say that whenever I grow as a person, I give my employees and the entire company permission to grow as well.

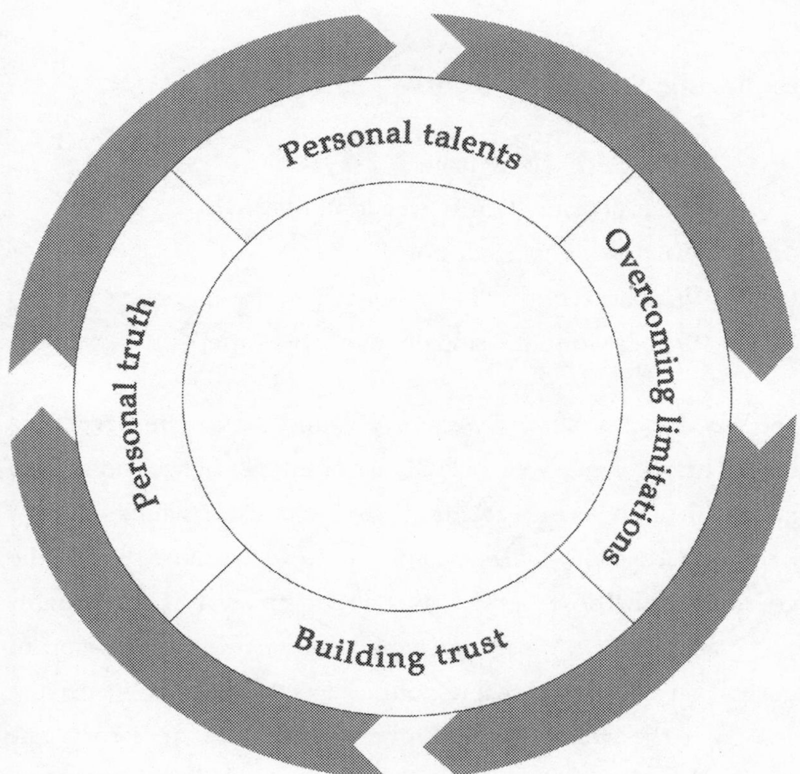

Figure 7: Cycle of the Chief

Before change can happen and become visible in the company, the first step is the chief's journey. It is a journey into the past and into the present.

The Journey into the Past

Going back into your own past has several goals: you can explore your own roots, discover your (partly) hidden fears and shadows; you can heal wounds from your childhood and discover your own possibilities.

Exploring Your Own Roots

Where do I come from?
What does my family tree look like?
What is my family's story?
Which strengths did I inherit from my ancestors?
Which wounds made my ancestors suffer?

We all became what we are. We, and those who have gone before us, always have a story. If we think about wounds of the past, war often springs to mind, the wounds of which can still be very active. *Self-actualization*: that word was not part of the vocabulary in those days. It was about survival. The thoughts and emotions of the past are handed down from generation to generation and are still shaping our leaders today. Now we need to recognize the wealth we have inherited from our ancestors. The knowledge we have acquired. The strengths we have developed.

Let us make peace with our heritage. Let us accept it in all of its facets: *What did my family and my ancestors do that fills me with deep gratitude?*

Exploring Your Own Fears and Shadows

> What is holding me back in my personal development?
> Which thought patterns and beliefs are a hindrance to me?

We all know them, those inner voices that keep us from realizing our ideas in our personal or professional lives. There is always someone whispering in our ear who feels that he needs to tell us right now that we are not good enough, not intelligent enough, not original enough, not fast enough, not … enough.

Enough!

Over the years, these inner voices have become our constant companions—like loyal soldiers. They have protected us our whole life, so that we wouldn't get hurt, so that we wouldn't rub anyone the wrong way or embarrass ourselves. They had good reasons (what could those be?), and they did their job very well.

But now the war is over. They are free to leave. We can discharge them with honors and give them a medal. Thank you. And now onward to new experiences!

Healing Childhood Wounds

> What was good about my childhood?
> What hurt?
> What is still making me angry?
> Which childhood fears are still plaguing me?

Our childhood left all of us with scars on our souls. Some of us have more than others. Some events have embedded themselves deep into our consciousness and still influence our thoughts and actions today, often in professional situations in which the decisions have nothing to do with the events of our childhood. Healing the inner child is an essential step in finding your own center and being able to think and act regardless of the opinion or approval of others. (Yes, even managers have an inner child.)

Ute Küffner puts it quite frankly: "There are many hurt children in companies, managers who have never dealt with their own personalities and whose actions are driven by power, approval, avoidance, fear." This is the difference to the way a chief acts. The chief has dealt with his own issues.

She advises her clients to look deeper. Recognize your own mechanisms and listen to your heart. That is where you will find the truth. Use this life to grow and become mature in all aspects, in all highs and lows. Look at your fear and recognize what it stands for. Know your own value, and live life to the fullest.

Exploring Your Own Possibilities

Most people have never had the time and space to explore their possibilities. Very early on, much too early, we are being prepared for the rat race: perform, be better, chase security rather than fun, and so on.

> What is in me?
> What do I have to de-clutter and let go?
> What would I like more of in my life?
> Which skills do I have to develop in order to achieve my goals and dreams, the professional and the personal ones?

With a good, responsible coach or therapist, you can work on all of these questions. The purpose is to recognize your own possibilities, to believe in them and integrate them into your everyday life, step by step.

Once we, as managers, have considered and worked on all of these aspects, we have traveled a long way on our path. We have journeyed into the past. So now what?

Well, now comes the now!

The Journey into the Present

Let's immerse ourselves into the present, into that which is with us in this moment, free from all thoughts of yesterday and tomorrow. The present is about radical self-care, about beauty, passion, and something that we often neglect: the wisdom of the crowds.

Radical Self-Care

Radical self-care, which is taking care of yourself without conditions or reservations, means to ask yourself the following questions on a regular basis:

> Do I accept myself as I am? Really?
> Do I take care of my body? Do I take enough time for myself? Am I building a relationship with myself like the one I have with my best friend?
> What can I do for myself?
> What do I really want out of life?

You are the most important person in your life. Nobody can take better care of you and protect you better. We have left our childhood behind and acquired the necessary skills to live and survive. Once we understand this and give ourselves love and recognition, others can truly see us, love us, and appreciate us. It is a universal law that we attract into our lives the things we do to ourselves.

Finding Your Own Beauty

Looking for beauty and our lives means to focus on the pleasant and nice things.

> What is beautiful to me? In myself, my body, my thoughts, my character, my view of the world, the world?
> Which people do I like having around me; what are good relationships for me? What images touch my spirit and my heart?

How would I like to live, how would I like to look, how would I like to move?

Beauty shows itself as radiance. Beautiful things and beautiful people have a presence that attracts us, almost like magic. Only those who have their own radiance and see beauty in themselves and others are able to help others grow and shine.

Elisabeth Kübler-Ross says, "Beautiful people are not born. People become beautiful once they have seen their deepest depth and went through them."

Kindling Your Own Passion

Passion has many facets.

What drives me? What makes me get up in the morning?
What excites me?
What do I like to do?
What amazes me?
What would I like to be a part of?
What do I want to leave this world?
When we know what drives us, we are able to give impetus to others!

Ute Küffner has a fitting description. "I want to live my life so that I am able to say: I have lived my own self, I have explored possibilities, I have created chances. I was scared to death. I was desperate. I was happy beyond measure."

Trusting the Wisdom of the Crowds

If you know where you stand and what makes you strong, you can embrace co-creation in a team and trust the wisdom of the crowds to do its part.

> Where do I stand with my knowledge?
> What do I need in order to see the big picture?
> Is my strategy really the best?
> Who can I ask? Who can I get on board?

The journeys into the past and present do not happen overnight. They are two processes that end in the center of the chief's soul. The chief looked in the mirror, plunged deep into his own personality, and is now acting from his center—not driven by power or fear like before.

The result is authenticity instead of authority—knowing you own values and skills, but also your own shadows.

The other three cycles can only be activated when the leader no longer stands in his own way, vying for attention. If the chief is centered, others are the center of attention. It creates a safe environment for the employees and the entire company to evolve and bloom.

> "The secret of a good team lies in the secure knowledge that the whole team has the full support of every member. I am very fortunate to have landed in such a team."
>
> –Sabrina Oberortner,
> DIE ERSTE GEIGE GmbH

* * *

It is important to understand that the journeys into the past and present create a foundation. But they are not the end of the chief's journey around the medicine wheel. A chief's fundamental attitude is to embrace ongoing personal growth.

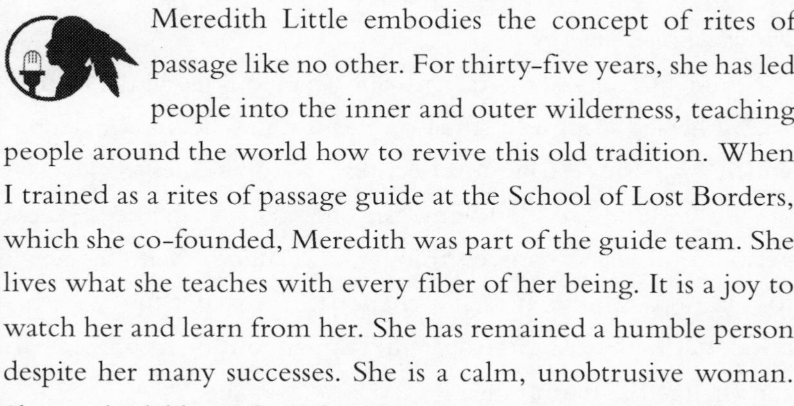

Meredith Little embodies the concept of rites of passage like no other. For thirty-five years, she has led people into the inner and outer wilderness, teaching people around the world how to revive this old tradition. When I trained as a rites of passage guide at the School of Lost Borders, which she co-founded, Meredith was part of the guide team. She lives what she teaches with every fiber of her being. It is a joy to watch her and learn from her. She has remained a humble person despite her many successes. She is a calm, unobtrusive woman. She speaks deliberately. What she says is so clear and powerful that her words never fail to touch me.

Meredith compares the personal growth of corporate leaders with a relationship. When we are young, we look for our opposite, someone who ostensibly "completes" us and compensates weak spots in our own wheel. However, a healthy relationship can function only if both partners know where they stand—if they have a balanced wheel or are aware of its power, at least—and do not try to complete each other but instead support each other in their own selves.

How many managers are looking for employees who seem to complete them but are really just covering the weak spots in the manager's personality? A very large number, I think. This strategy does not create a sound structure. It is not surprising that the people involved often use the dynamics of power and powerlessness to prevent the house of cards from tumbling.

Every winter, Meredith takes some time off for quiet reflection. She questions everything she does, even now that she is in her early sixties with more than thirty-five years of experience as a professional rites of passage guide. She says that she still has some self-doubt and asks herself, *Are the things I do in this world good enough?*

Meredith does not stand still. She keeps looking in the mirror, asking herself if a given situation needs a new focus. In winter, which is a good season for reflection, she sometimes spends days on end without talking to anyone. She says that she needs these periods of silence to process things and realign herself. She needs to withdraw to give herself a chance to think not just with her mind, but with her heart, too. Only things coming from the heart can change the world, she says.

What would our world be like if all corporate leaders were capable of such humility? What would our world be like if all managers questioned their own actions and their consequences for the world so thoroughly?

There is a story about Nelson Mandela, who was once asked how he was able to survive prison for so long. "I prepared for my task," he said. He knew that he would be free one day and lead his people. In prison, he learned Afrikaans. He reflected on himself and his country. He prepared.

"Being a manager means learning to hear what my task is," says Ute Küffner.

What is your task? How do you prepare for it?

The Second Cycle: Cycle of the Employee (Hero's Journey)

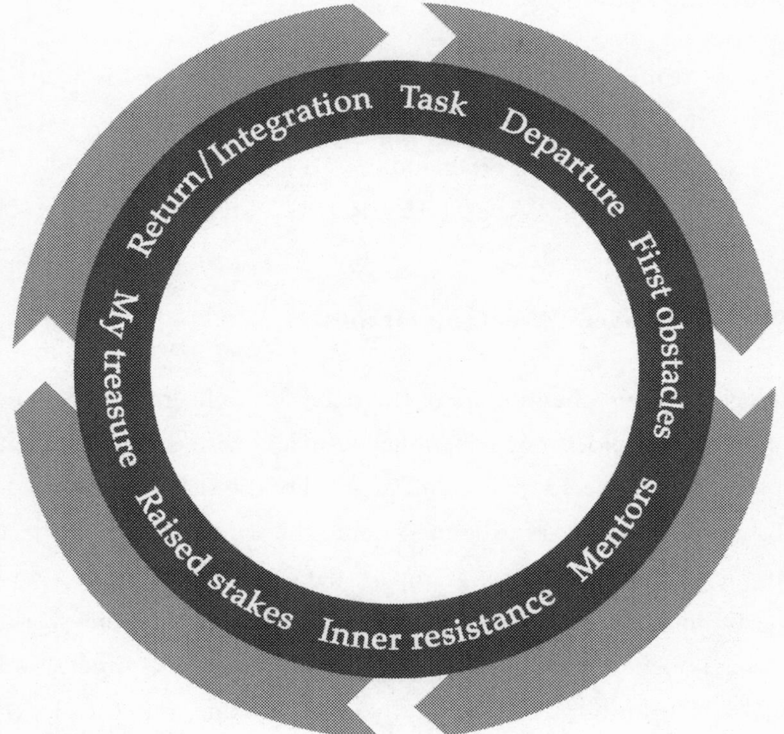

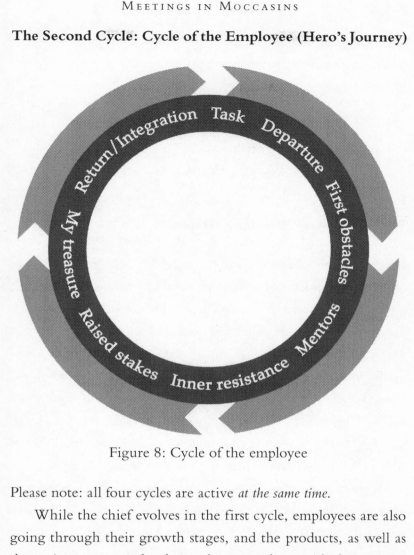

Figure 8: Cycle of the employee

Please note: all four cycles are active *at the same time.*

While the chief evolves in the first cycle, employees are also going through their growth stages, and the products, as well as the entire company, develop and mature along with them.

One fact that most companies neglect to consider or simply overlook is that sustainable corporate growth can be achieved only if there is a sound foundation for the chief and the tribe.

If the chief is not centered with access to his full potential and if the employees are unaware of their own development, highs and lows, victories and defeats, the other cycles cannot be activated—or they do not provide the best possible results.

> "Our teamwork at DIE ERSTE GEIGE is especially valuable for my life, because we appreciate each other and share a sense of humor."
> –Brigitte Weber, DIE ERSTE GEIGE GmbH

Why Employees Are True Heroes

In the old days, the hunters of the tribe were cheered as they set out into the wilderness. When they returned with their prey, even more cheers greeted them. The survival of the tribe was secured. Today, the hunters are still sent out into the wild—into the project jungle. It is hot in there, cramped, dangerous—and after a few yards, most hunters cannot breathe anymore, let alone work. Instead of cheers, we find sore employees, critical customers, and shaky IT solutions that don't really satisfy anyone, yet cost a lot of money. In most cases, the root cause of this is not found in those peachy, well-considered methods, but on the human level.

If we look at old myths and heroic sagas passed on through the generations without losing any of their relevance, we see that they are all based on certain basic patterns. Mythologists like Joseph Campbell studied these patterns. They call them the "hero's journey." Native Americans call it a quest or a rite of passage.

On his journey, the hero goes through certain growth phases that take him closer to his goal—after testing his heart, mind, and strength, of course. A true hero must suffer before he can return, victorious, to his people.

We still have heroes today. Let's call them "project heroes." They are the millions and billions of employees and managers all over the world who make projects happen every day.

1. The Call: The Hero Receives a Task

The cell phone rings. "Barbara, we need you now!" A customer is in crisis. An IT solution is producing nothing but errors. The customer's customers are complaining. All emergency measures have failed or made matters worse. Now they want me to fix it.

2. Refusal: The Hero Hesitates

The task is precarious. Can I do it? Do I want to? Couldn't they find anyone else? Of course not; nobody wants to touch this thing. If I mess up, there will be consequences for other projects and my team.

3. Departure: The Hero Begins His Journey

Fine, I'll do it. If I approach this analytically, it could work. It will all work out. Self-motivation is everything.

4. Trials: Initial Problems Occur

Well, the analytical approach didn't help. How do I even get all departments to the table? It's a madhouse, as always! And everybody is annoyed with this issue, because things have not been working for weeks. Now what?

5. The Mentor: The Hero Receives Support from People or Inner Resources

Light at the end of the tunnel. The senior manager of the department has my back. His faith in me makes the others trust me. The meetings are much more relaxed now. Take a deep breath and wade in. In between: recharge in nature, my source of strength. And meditation. Those two things keep me going.

6. The First Threshold: The Hero Wrestles with Inner Resistance

I'm beginning to get the picture. The project history is clear, as are the error types. But this thing is taking on huge dimensions. Can I even do it? Regular meetings with my coach are helping me keep the big picture in mind and change perspectives every once in a while. He reminds me of the truly important things.

7. More Trials: The Hero Is Challenged and Draws Strength from His Inner Resources

Some days, I feel like a beaten dog. Before the first wound can even be stitched up, the next blow draws blood again. What do I touch first without doing even more damage? I remember my favorite TV show, *House.* Like Dr. House, I withdraw with the project team to an empty room, take a flip chart, and collectively think. The patient, or rather, the project, is dying. What does it need to survive? Slowly, solutions appear. We capture them on the flip chart.

8. Transformation: The Hero Receives the Treasure

Progress! Small steps, but still. But it is less about methods and more about humans: developing a feeling for all people involved, asking the right questions, using skills and talents in the best way, trusting my intuition, motivating others. As a team, we go to a carnival. We eat, laugh, and buy a project mascot, a pink balloon pig. The pig becomes our trademark. For every mistake, one team member has to walk through the entire department carrying the pig. The embarrassment motivates the whole team to work hard on not making mistakes anymore. Once again, my sense of humor and my intuition prove to be my greatest treasures.

9. Refusal of Return: The Hero Does Not Want to Go Back

Suddenly, everything is running smoothly. No errors anywhere. And now it's all over? But we just got started! And more importantly, what will happen with the next project? Which battles do I have to fight there?

10. Farewell: The Hero Has No Choice but to Return

More optimization is simply not possible. Everything is smooth and shiny. No reason for me to stay. I can go. After a year. It's a strange feeling.

11. The Return: The Hero Crosses the Threshold into His Ordinary Life

The last meeting, where the results are presented. Everybody praises my efforts, and I am told that I don't have to be present at the meetings anymore. It's the sudden end of a journey in which I invested a lot of energy and heart.

12. Master of Two Worlds: The Hero Shared His New Knowledge with His Community

All that new knowledge needs to be integrated into our everyday work life. As a team, we talk about the experiences. I am happy and grateful that everything worked out so well. And I realize that ordinary projects are not interesting enough anymore. I want to do things that challenge me professionally and as a person. And then, out of the blue, the next project turns up. The journey begins again. Can I do it? Do I want to?

This is an example of a hero's journey that unfolds along the growth stages and comes to an end in the sense of the mythical hero's journey. However, the reality often looks very different. Sometimes project teams get stuck in an endless loop in stages one through four. When the first problem comes their way, they give up and go back to stage one. It is a game of project Monopoly. Other teams make it to stage six before crashing, because they lack self-reflection. The truly successful teams go through all stages—with all pains and laurels. These laurels have to be handled with care, though.

Hero's Journey Instead of Heroics: The Subtle Difference

You are only as good as your next success. There are many heroes out there who master huge projects by themselves every day. Usually, as their successes multiply, their egos swell, too. "I did it all by myself (pat on the back); it's all mine and I won't share with anyone!"

A true project hero understands that it is not about heroics. It is about the hero's journey, which means: yes, I am going alone. I have my adventure. And then I share with my colleagues what I have learned along the way. This is how my personality evolves and my strength grows. This does not just make me more successful; it makes all of us more successful.

From Hounded to Celebrated: Do These Old Rituals Have a Place in Modern Companies?

In many project teams, burnout is a regular occurrence. We all go through the hero's journey every day without even knowing it! The rituals of this journey are long forgotten. We do not go through the archaic, natural cycle anymore; we rush through it. It's the rat race.

The following ideas of the hero's journey can help with reviving the natural cycle in our companies today, thus creating true heroes who do what they need to do and feel good about it—and stay healthy.

Witnesses: The Cheering Crowds

The beginning and end of a journey need to be clearly defined. Otherwise, the boundaries blur and success is no longer perceived, because it coincides with the next stumbling block in the neighboring project. How about designating part of the team to send the project hero off with good wishes and welcome him home with cheers? That way, the project has a cleanly defined beginning and a clear end, which allows the employee to free up energy for new tasks.

Active Listening: Much More Than Small Talk

The buzz around the water cooler and in the cafeteria proves every day that we have a deep-seated need for stories. What would happen if we told those stories in a structured context instead of in passing by the coffeemaker? What if we reserve a period for just listening and acknowledging and appreciating the "treasures" (e.g., milestones, results) people bring? Employees who are truly seen heard and appreciated develop heroic powers.

Inner Resources: Safety Belts for a Steep Ascent

Many people are not aware of their own strength and value. Who am I? What can I do? What holds me back? What can help me in standing firm? What can I fall back on when things get tough? Knowing your own resources gives you the strength and assurance to fully commit to a project. Which person on the team (or from the outside) can be asked to reinforce these resources?

Found Treasures: Symbols of Growth

On every journey, we find something on the inside or outside to bring home. How can each team member be enabled to name his or her found treasures, thus expressing his or her personal growth? And how can we truly conclude a project—not just on paper? How can we give it a clean ending, and what could be a symbol for it?

By integrating such simple elements, which are not going to take much time or cost much money, we strengthen not just each individual but the entire project team. We can satisfy deeply human needs, bring to light untapped potential, and create a dynamic that makes the project a true success for everybody involved.

The myth is alive. Whether we like it or not—we are heroes. Let's begin our journey!

> "DIE ERSTE GEIGE turns every project into something special. This motivates me to give my very best every time, and looking back, I marvel

at the things I was able to achieve. Thank you for that!

–Sabine Faltmann, PR Liaison
DIE ERSTE GEIGE GmbH

The Third Cycle: The Innovation Cycle

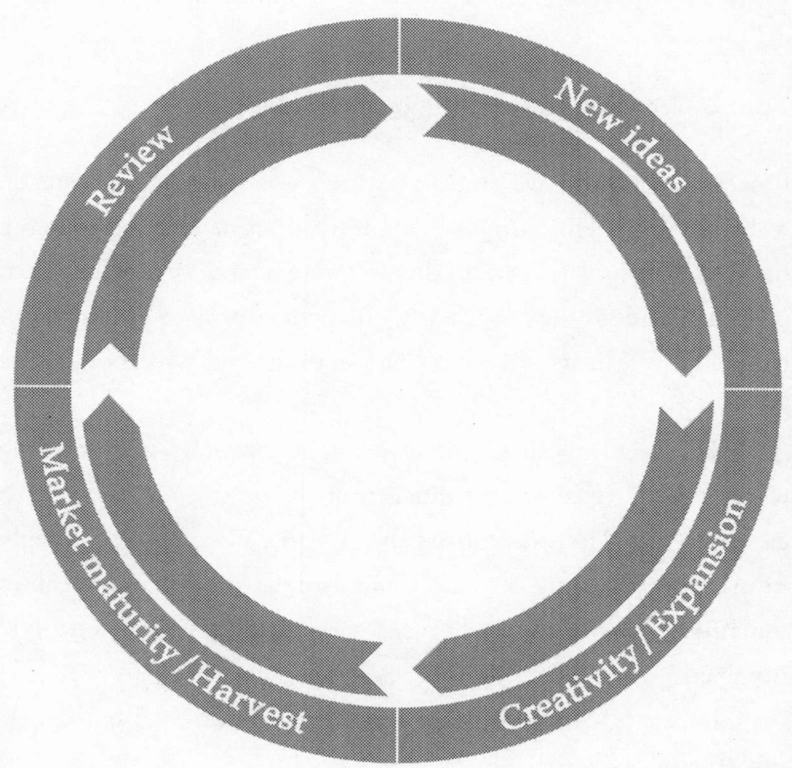

Figure 9: The four quarters of the innovation cycle

Nature "ticks" in quarters, of course: spring, summer, fall, winter. A time to sow, a time to grow, a time to harvest, and a time to rest and gather strength.

Wrapped up in today's constant hype, we forget that everything has its time in life. We produce around the clock; we are global and always available, permanently wired. Nothing in nature works this way. No apple tree bears fruit all year long, just because we tell it to be more productive. Gain a competitive edge in the orchard and become a farmer's-market leader!

We keep sowing, sowing, and sowing; harvesting, harvesting, and harvesting without respecting or even paying any attention to the phases between them. In other words, we keep planting ideas for products and services in our orchard without having a concept for preparing and nurturing the soil, without a clue of nature, the source and fertile ground for our seedling that we want to grow big (better yet, huge!) and strong (mega-strong!) as quickly as possible.

Let's stay with the apple tree. A tree needs time to grow and bear fruit. And a person needs time to grow as well. Along with its people, a company needs time to grow, too!

> "When the company grows too fast, the people cannot keep up with it—and then the company shrinks again."
>
> –Theo Knaus

Ute Küffner expresses similar thoughts: "My time as a corporate manager was deadline-driven. One project after the other, one reorganization phase after the other. People are deprived of the harvest, and things do not make sense anymore."

What does make sense, which "quarterly goals" does an apple tree have in the course of its year of growth, and how can they be applied to a corporate setting?

Spring is the time to sow. We place the seed in the earth or go to the best nursery we know to purchase a young apple tree with a trunk no thicker than a sausage.

We let our imagination and creativity run free, looking for new ideas, brainstorming with the team and alone. It is the time for continued education and for unfolding our potential. We create more space to think, organize workshops about new product ideas, and think about ways to maintain and expand on our uniqueness. It is also a time for promotions. Which employee is able to move up to the next level—with proper acknowledgement and celebration of his achievements thus far?

Apart from setting and meeting sales goals, coming up with new product or service ideas could be another goal. At the end of the quarter, these ideas are evaluated to determine which should be pursued further.

Summer is the time to move. The ideas have been planted. Now the little tree needs to be fertilized and watered; it needs to soak up enough sunshine and light to reach its full height. The trunk is getting thicker and stronger every day. And while new branches and shoots grow above the ground, up into the sky, the tree is also deepening and widening its roots to stand firm in any wind and weather. And one day, the blossoms will turn into fruit—green, at first, and sour enough to make your mouth pucker (like projects and ideas "harvested" too soon). Later, the fruit will be fat and red and juicy—fresh and crunchy, as only fruit plucked straight from the tree can be.

In terms of our products and services, this means that we develop three of the newly generated ideas to the prototype stage. Which specific nutrients and fertilizers does each of them need? How much warmth—or heart—do they need, and from what sources? What are their strengths? Where are their roots giving them strength and a firm hold; where are the branches that give the whole thing radiance and globality?

Fall is the time to harvest. Now we can pick and enjoy our apples! Some, we eat right there, under the tree; some, we save for later. We give thanks for the results, even if not all of them match our expectations. And if we look closely, we might even find some unexpected fruit on our tree. Thanks!

Our products and services are now ready to be introduced into the market.

And then comes winter. Time to review and gather our strength. The tree withdraws its sap. The leaves fall in order to become part of the nurturing soil for next year. Things that are not ripe by now will not ripen this year. Things that have not been harvested yet will not be added to the store.

In our company, we turn to the inside. What worked out this year? What was great? What missed the mark or remained green or unused? What can we do even better next time? How can we expand our product and talent portfolio? Which decisions have to be made, which gaps filled? Who deserves gratitude and honors? We define the individual measures to be taken in spring—and then we let go, no longer looking back but focusing our attention calmly forward, secure in the knowledge that the cycle will renew itself and that there is nothing left to do for us.

Quarters with a Seasonal Rhythm

As an experienced entrepreneur, I can say that the more aware I am of the "four seasons," the more I try to time our business activities to coincide, the easier it is for my company to go through each development process, e.g., product development. In the first seven years, I was able to double—and in some cases, triple—our sales. The rhythm of these steps toward our success can be slower than desired or demanded by the business community, but it is organic and thus sustainable. My employees know how I think and go with the rhythm without needing daily reminders. Many things happen without words, rooted in our self-conception and attitude.

What do I do? I formulate a vision for the year and use it as a basis to determine the goals for each quarter. Once per quarter, we meet as a team to reflect on the current situation and to adapt our business activities for the next quarter, if necessary. We have found that this approach makes strenuous marketing campaigns unnecessary. Things move better and faster, because we all pull together.

At the end of every quarter, I take a long weekend to review my experiences. And I conclude the quarter just for myself, often with a ritual. Long walks are part of these weekends. Native Americans call these "medicine walks." You start with a concrete question and walk toward the answer by embracing nature for a day or so. My question could be: What did I learn in this quarter?

On my walk, I am very aware of nature. I watch how nature is preparing for the next phase, the coming cycle. I learn by observation, note my insights in a diary, and use these quarterly observations for my annual review at the end of the year.

Quarterly Goals for the Employees

The personal goals of each individual are an essential part of the quarterly goals of the company.

Spring: Exploring Your Creativity

What did I like to do as a child; what was fun for me? Spring is the time to use your imagination and nurture your muse. We stimulate all senses to awaken our awareness from its winter sleep and sharpen our perception.

Summer: Reveling in the Abundance

Nature is glowing in all its glory. What does splendor mean to me; what is beauty? What do I like about me? How can I make my own beauty blossom? Now is the time to be active, to soak up the sun and go on adventures with friends and colleagues.

Fall: Time to Savor

What does the fullness of life mean to me? What am I grateful for in my life? What have I been able to harvest so far in my life? And what will this year's personal and professional harvest be? It is time to celebrate, to be joyful and share with others, to give something back. Which social project could I work for? Which person close to me could use my help for a while?

Winter: Withdrawing and Gathering Strength

Which stories does this year have to tell me? With whom can I share them? Which of my talents did I build on this year? Which energy stores did I deplete and need to refill now?

Day by day, month by month, we go through the seasons and the year. And in the course of our professional life, we go through the four "big quarters": trainee, team member, manager, elder.

Personally, I am looking forward to the day when "elder" becomes a corporate position!

> "I work with DIE ERSTE GEIGE on certain projects, and I always feel like a full member of the team. We treat each other with complete honesty, and I am able to voice my wishes and concerns. The focus is not on the bottom line, but on people with their talents, preferences and growth potential. I have never seen this in any other consulting firm."
>
> –Susanne Hache,
> Freelancer DIE ERSTE GEIGE GmbH

The Fourth Cycle: Cycle of the Company

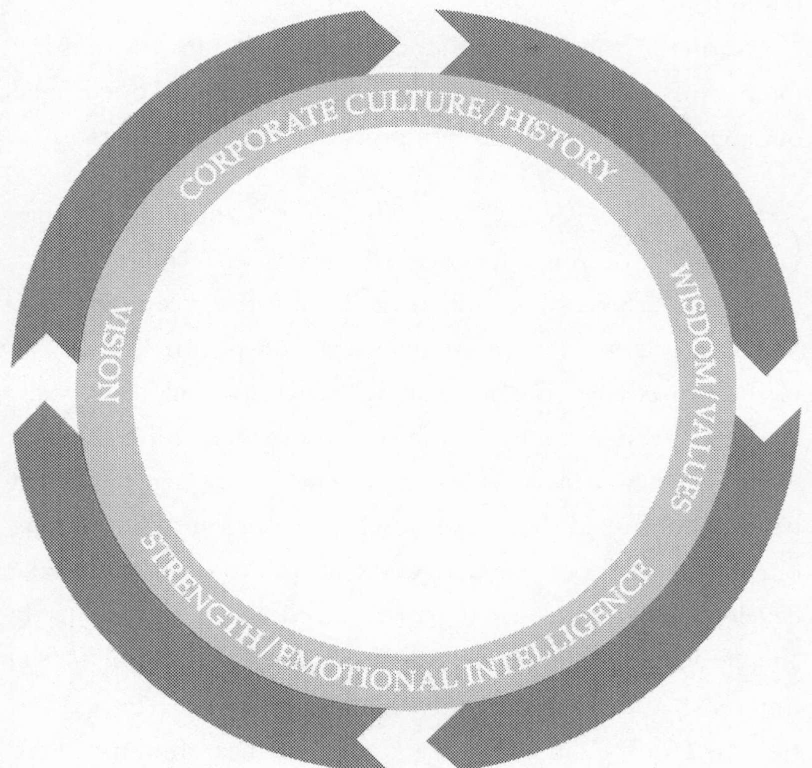

Figure 10: The cycle of the company

When the three other cycles are active and running smoothly, the fourth wheel is turning (almost) on its own. The values and wisdom of the entire company are lived every day, as a matter of course. The company is aware of its strengths and creates visions in a natural, organic, playful way—not with laborious flip charts and endless PowerPoint presentations that leave body, heart, mind, and soul cold. The corporate culture and company history are exciting and worth sharing—and they will stand the test of time.

Naturally, a multidimensional model such as this, with many intersecting and interacting parts, cannot be activated or changed overnight. Usually, this growth process takes several years.

Several years. Today, our way of thinking has very little room for such a long period. Things need to happen fast, and results need to be measurable fast. Where we used to have annual goals and planning cycles of twelve- to twenty-four months, we now have quarterly goals. We do not think in longer cycles anymore. Still, as Theo Knaus confirms, you cannot make long-term investments without having diminished short-term results! By constantly shortening our cycles, we limit our development options or, worse, make development impossible altogether. In order to grow sustainably and healthily, we need long-term rhythms. The term *rhythm* implies that we also need to look beyond the mere facts and figures. Thinking in numbers and scales is linear thinking in the sense of "I have a goal and need to reach it." We often overlook the fact that life continues beyond the goal and that the things to the left and right of our path are just as important if we want to reach our goal. Let's relearn to think in cycles.

It is not enough to go through these cycles once. The individual wheels work every day and all year long—in our company and in us as humans. Embracing change is a basic philosophy. Life as such and the life of a company need to be seen as something that is in constant flux. Life and death happen every day in our personal lives and in our professional lives. It is an unending cycle of letting go and being born. The more we can surrender ourselves to this state of flux, the more liberated we are—as a person, as a manager, as a brand.

* * *

The idea of the four cycles is just one of the many options and applications of the wheel of life. The points of the compass can also be assigned to archetypes, for instance. Some teachings of C. G. Jung are based on the approach described here. Books about the wheel of life (medicine wheel) and about the stages of human development offer a wealth of information and inspiration, if you would like to explore the subject further.

What we need to know is that these four cycles are completed over and over again, and that there is nothing in this world that can change this natural law—just like the seasons follow each other in the same order or like night always follows day.

This also means that we have a chance to work on the different aspects of the wheel: for ourselves, our team, and our projects. As in a spiral, each completed cycle lifts us up to the next level.

> "A great mix of a cordial, familiar atmosphere and target-oriented empowerment."
>
> –Claus Pflug,
>
> Freelancer at DIE ERSTE GEIGE GmbH

PART 3

The Tribe

CHAPTER 14

From the Concrete Teepee into the Wilderness: Why Companies and Employees Need a Vision

It is a hot day. The people who thought they would be taking a stroll and selected dress shoes and heels to wear have a problem. The Chief doesn't pay any attention to the moans and groans behind him. He is climbing up the grassy hill like a young Alpine goat.

"Are we there yet?" jokes a young sales manager.

"I need to pee," a colleague chimes in.

"Me, too, and I'm hungry," says a young woman. She is actually serious.

Since the arrival of The Chief, people have gotten used to open-air meetings. Today, they drove into the mountains—and each of them is supposed to spend part of the afternoon alone, without a cell phone, laptop, or anything else. For most team members, this is a horrifying thought! And what good does it do, anyway? What are they doing out here in the wilderness? Piles of work are waiting on their desks.

* * *

An Indian text says (loosely translated):

> "If a boy is not initiated into manhood, if he is not shaped by the skill and love of the elders, he will destroy the culture of his tribe. If the fire burning within him is not integrated into the heart of the community with care and love, it will burn down the tribe's structure, just to feel its own warmth."

This is still the point, even today: guiding the inner fire of the young, dynamic movers and shakers in the right direction, so that it can feed the corporate flame, not destroy it by flaring up briefly before dying—and possibly causing damage.

One of the oldest rituals in Native American tradition that marks and prepares the way for the transition from adolescence to adulthood is the vision quest.

Supervised by a medicine man or woman, the seeker is sent to a remote area for three to four days. Left to his own devices, his place in life, his talents, strengths, and weaknesses, his life's work and contribution to the community will be revealed to him during this time. The seeker fasts to keep his mind and body empty and clear, ready for the thoughts and insights coming to him during these days.

The seeker selects a spot for his time in the wilderness, which is marked with a stone circle. The circle represents the wheel of life, the sacred cycle of all things, as well as the four directions and the four elements: fire, water, earth, and air. The "blue" and "red" paths of life meet in the circle: wisdom and power. The last stone that completes the circle stands for the door to the east. Once this door is closed, the seeker sits in the wheel of life for three days.

These three days are not easy. Apart from a range of weather conditions challenging the seeker, he is confronted with his worst fears: his pride, his stubbornness, and his limits. At the end of his journey into his self, he knows who he is. And he recognizes that we are all part of a vast cycle. He started with *I* and arrived at *we*.

A seeker returning from the wilderness feels like a new man. Previously, he wandered through his life, dying a symbolical death in order to rise again. Now he carries within himself the four aspects of life that make him whole as a person: his strength, his wisdom, his emotions, and the wisdom of his ancestors. And he has found his vision—in his heart, not his mind. Native Americans say that only visions coming from the heart follow the Beauty Way. A vision based on the desire to control others or rooted in greed goes against the natural order of things.

A seeker coming home from his vision quest was greeted with great joy by the community and celebrated as a hero, because he had the courage to look into his own soul.

What Exactly Is a Vision?

A vision is an ideal of the future. It reveals the things that make our company unique. It shows our *raison d'être* (reason for existing) in this world. It is the idea of the things we will have achieved with our company in the future and of the way we will treat ourselves and others. The vision gives us meaning, because it provides answers to the question of "What?"—and, more importantly, to the question of "Why?"

Many companies put their vision into words in great detail. Personally, I prefer collages, like the Dream Board. A vision does not contain instructions on how to reach it. Those are figured out during other planning phases. The vision is a guideline that helps us make decisions in order to stay on our path. And it is an intention to which we commit even in challenging times, when other paths would lead to success more quickly and easily.

If I have a vision in my personal life that I will have more time for my family and hobbies and to plant the garden of my dreams in five years, I know which steps I need to take *today* to get there.

If a company knows exactly where it wants to be in five or ten years, its people are able to determine *today* which customers and partners to attract and who to hire.

Personally, I prefer the term *guiding principle.* A guiding principle comprises, apart from the goal, a set of basic values for the company.

In my opinion, a guiding principle contains

- the vision;
- the mission;
- the desired corporate culture; and
- guidelines.

Let's stay with the vision. Some companies have a five-year vision, others a ten- or twenty-year vision. No matter which timeframe we choose, we need this guide, personally and in our business life, to find our inner and outer direction.

Naturally, everything is moving constantly. In a community, in a tribe, the guiding principle, and thus the vision, may change. People live. Guiding principles live. Visions live. It is a good idea to reexamine our goals every once in a while. Are we still going in the right direction?

What Are the Criteria for a Vision That Works?

- Everybody needs to understand and support the vision. All people involved want to be part of the vision!
- The vision has meaning and offers a common focal point for the company and all employees.
- The vision energizes the company and all employees.
- The vision conveys an image of the future of the company and all employees.
- The vision is based on shared values.
- The vision is unique.
- The vision is honest. It is not just about looking good, but also about doing good.
- The vision is so big that it can only be achieved together.
- And the vision is alive. It cannot just exist on paper, but must be shared and experienced every day.

How Can We Go on a Vision Quest Today, in a Modern Business Setting?

The greatest gift a vision quest adapted to the corporate world has to offer is the discovery of a company's *uniqueness on the market.* We find what makes us strong, now and always—no matter what happens in the outside world.

This kind of "corporate vision quest" is great for people on the board of directors or a leadership team. It might not be possible to sit in a stone circle for three to four days (just imagine the chairman's cell phone ringing and he cannot get to it, because it is outside of the circle!).

But a change of scene is certainly possible—perhaps a city none of the participants has ever visited or a remote place in the country where everybody can truly relax.

I would like to offer you three possible formats for a vision quest. Each consists of three phases:

1. Preparation
2. Vision quest/threshold
3. Return

During the *preparation* period, the current life and work situation needs to be examined: Where am I? Which transition is coming up? Native Americans begin this time by fasting and performing certain tasks in nature, ceremonies, and rituals. They also use the time to find the place where the seeker will spend his time alone.

The *vision quest* itself usually takes four days and nights. The seeker visits the selected place alone, without bringing any food. He just has his bedroll and a tarp to protect him from sun, wind, rain, and cold. It is a time in which we use all our senses to experience our surroundings, in which we become one with the world and find the clarity we seek.

The seeker leaves the wilderness or secluded spot, *returns* to the community, and breaks the fast. He tells the group about his personal experiences and listens to their stories. All acknowledge the insights found by each seeker. They determine how the new experiences can be integrated into their lives, the group of seekers parts company, each of them returning to his world stronger and with newfound clarity.

Here are the three possible formats:

Business Quest (Three Days): In the City, No More Than Twelve Participants

A business quest is the perfect way to answer the following questions:

- How did we experience personal growth this year or this quarter?
- What did we achieve?
- Which experiences enriched our lives?
- From which experiences did we learn—and in what way?
- Did we stick to our principles?
- Where does our journey lead us? What is important to us in the coming year? How do we feel about this year?
- What are the next steps?
- Which images could stand for these results (in creating a shared Dream Board, for example)?

Once a year, I spend a long weekend with my team in a beautiful place. This weekend is always a combination of community and being alone, self-reflection and sharing, city and country, slow and quick-paced.

We look for places in natural surroundings to talk to each other, sit in a circle, and share things. Professional things often mingle with personal stories in these conversations; it is impossible to draw a clean line. Passers-by might think that it is strange how we are sitting in a city park, with a flip chart and everything. But it has been our experience that these conversations in a strange place, in an unusual setting, are the ones that touch us the most. We are switching perspectives on all levels.

A business quest works best if it has no more than twelve participants. In SMEs, the participants could be employees from the different departments. In bigger companies, this quest is ideal for the board of directors or the leadership team.

If the goal is to define the company's guiding principle or resolve deeper issues, three days are not enough. These things are better suited for a team quest or a leadership quest.

Team Quest (Five Days): At a Conference Hotel Outside of the City

The group journeys through the four essential aspects of life or business:

1. Strength: What does our company stand for? Where do we see the potential of our employees, products, and services?

2. Wisdom: Which ideas shape our corporate culture? How do we meet today's challenges? How do we treat our employees?
3. Emotions: Which emotions do we evoke in our customers? How do we improve the life and attitude of every single person we meet, e.g., customers, suppliers, and partners?
4. Wisdom of our ancestors: What do we see in the history of our company since its foundation? Which obstacles did we have to overcome? How did we accomplish that? Who are the great role models among former managing directors and managers? Which of their values and insights can we use today?

As part of this journey, all participants have to spend some time between dawn and dusk all by themselves to reflect on the things that are important to them.

The insights gained on such a five-day team quest can be extraordinary. If we don't just "sweet talk" but really dive in and face the truth, if we allow conflicts and emotions—the ones we often suppress in our concrete teepees—to come to the surface, we can build a foundation for true innovation and a healthy working atmosphere. We can clarify and strengthen our existing paths and find completely new ones. This is when the corporate vision is flooded with clarity and drive of the kind that could never be created in a gray, uninspiring conference room.

At the same time, the shared ritual reveals personal strengths, values, and talent of each individual, which we often overlook in our busy business life.

Leadership Quest (Seven Days): In Nature, No More Than Seven Participants

Another format I adapted for our modern world is one for a company's decision-makers, the chiefs. Once a year, you should take the time to look inside. Evaluate where you stand. Work on the best and the not-so-great parts of yourself. Let your soul mature a bit, so that you are truly empowered to lead a team. Don't just talk about good things; do them.

The leadership quest is a journey through the medicine wheel, through your own four seasons. You explore your own life situation and discover your desires and fears.

Each participant spends twenty-four hours alone. Outdoors. Without food, just equipped with a bedroll, tarp and water. You could say that this journey goes back to basics, inside and out.

The last phase of the journey is about integration. It is very important that you integrate your experience into your everyday life. Every participant of a leadership quest now has a clear and strong vision of his own roots, his values, and his personal life's dream.

Antje von Dewitz (VAUDE) confirms my experience, saying, "When we take our employees on nature tours, we touch them directly, without any facades. In nature, people are authentic and tap into their full power."

I also recommend regular periods of introspection for individuals. Throughout the year, take time for some days of silence. Take trip to a place where you are alone and unreachable—and don't bring work. Spend time with yourself, and think about the following questions, perhaps while writing or hiking:

- Am I in the right place?
- Do I have a job that does not just pay the bills, but also gives me joy?
- Can I use all of my talents and my full potential in my job?
- What would I like to integrate into my professional life?
- Which talents and skills can I use and develop in my personal life?
- If I didn't have to worry about money (no family, no mortgage, etc.), which job would I like to do?
- What is my goal for the end of the year?
- What are my goals in five, ten, and twenty years?
- At the end of my life, which achievements do I want to remember?

Find the courage to look deep into your soul, your thoughts, emotions, even your deep convictions, as well as your limitations. I promise, it will be worth the effort!

Something for your medicine bag: What could stand for your personal vision? Take an hour, half a day, or a day to be surrounded by nature—and let it give you the right answers and symbols.

Results of your medicine walk, with the subject "My Vision":

CHAPTER 15

Common Sense: Developing a Sense of Community

The entire team is tense. A customer unexpectedly cancelled a big project. What happened? Who made a mistake? The departments have been at war with each other for days. Everybody blames everybody else for the failure. And all look to The Chief, as he enters the conference room last. As usual, the people on his left and right make room for his warbonnet. Before sitting down, he bends over the table, opens his hand, and lets a big spider crawl across the tabletop.

"What can we learn from this spider?" The Chief asks, looking at everybody in the room.

"That the customer is the spider and we are the fly?" says a young colleague in resignation.

"Not quite," says The Chief. "The spider shows us that we need a web."

* * *

In 2012, I attended the annual conference of the European Council Network (ENC) in the Netherlands. In a discussion on the subject of "community," we talked about the meaning of the concept of *community*. From that discussion, I concluded the following:

- Community is a safe space in which to grow and nurture my talents.
- Community is sharing space, time, and values.
- Community is a balance between "together" and "alone."
- Community works with common sense—using all our senses to relate to others.
- Community is being held and understood in all work and life situations. It is support without the expectation of an immediate quid pro quo.
- Community is based on a healthy give and take.
- Community is having common roots in a vision (the inner fire), within the group, and within the individual.
- Community is a network of possibilities and talents.
- Community means growing together, with all negative and positive aspects.
- Community is not closed off, but open to the outside and ready to integrate partners and customers.
- Community is a world that can comprise many other worlds. But not just anyone can arbitrarily enter this world. A newcomer needs to fit into the big picture in order to be successfully integrated (narrow-door policy).

For Native Americans, *community* meant a certain order and clarity—maintaining relationships with the other members of the tribe and with nature, too. Without this shared foundation of the community, survival would have been difficult. The group ensured the continued existence by hunting together, maintaining the tents, caring for the animals.

One person would not have been able to have all necessary talents. But in the group, everybody was able to focus on the things he or she did best. Therefore, every individual had the opportunity to grow and nurture his or her talents without being constantly afraid of being kicked out by another member of the tribe.

Community may have a different meaning in our world. The communities we form today are probably based on different values. However, communities do have some universal characteristics:

- Seeing and being seen, making talents visible
- Supporting and nurturing young people
- Elders maintaining and passing on traditions
- Speaking and listening with our hearts, not just our minds
- Treating each other with care and respect

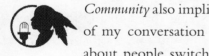

Community also implies longer duration. I am thinking of my conversation with Theo Knaus, who talked about people switching jobs every few years—job-hopping. Theo said, correctly, that people who have short-term success do not have to deal with the long-term consequences of their work. If I work in a position for three years before switching jobs, I just have to be successful for three years. I leave an organization that is bled dry and really needs some time to regenerate and restructure. I leave all of this to my successor, who does not know the team or may have different goals he needs to achieve. This is not sustainable. And nobody gets to have a very important experience. Community reaches beyond short-term success.

Katja Rück is a psychologist from Berlin who works mainly with groups and their processes. In council, she found a very efficient tool for her work with groups. The experience and sense of community are different if you sit in a circle. "A group is more than the sum of its parts," says Katja. She often uses nature as a model, observing natural processes and transferring her observations to her group work.

At the ECB conference in the Netherlands, it was her idea to compare building a community with building a spiderweb. For expert advice on how to draw a spider and its web, she asked Merle, an eleven-year-old girl who also attended the event. Merle listened quietly and drew pictures while we talked. At the end of the day, she summarized our often-lengthy council talks in a few words. Most of the time, she nailed it.

The wonderful combination of a child's inquiring mind and an adult's idea created a great metaphor. Katja kindly gave me permission to use it here to describe the dynamic in business teams. On the following pages, you will find Katja's and Merle's "community blueprint."

Applied to Our Company, What Does *Community* Mean?

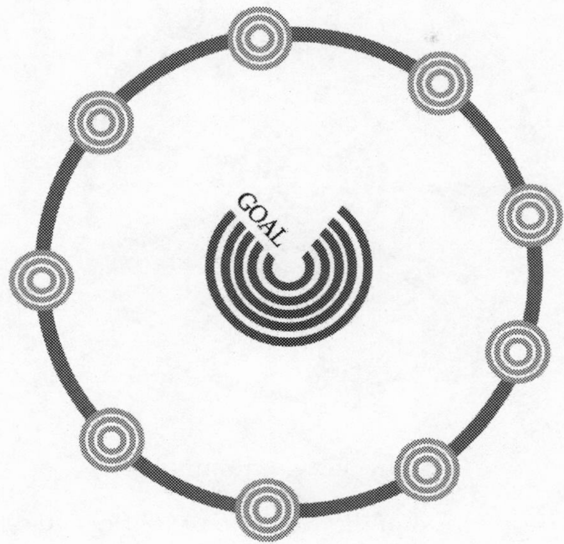

Figure 11: Community

Gather motivated and open people in your company. Work together on a guiding principle that will light the fire in every individual and forge a connection to the inner fire of the company.

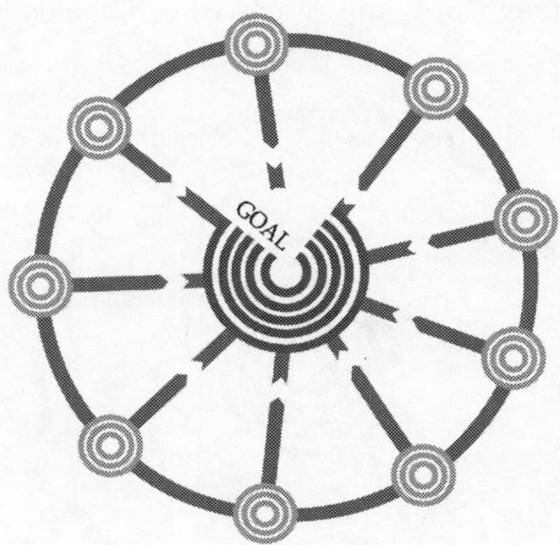

Figure 12: Community

This is the basic thread of the web of possibilities and talents.

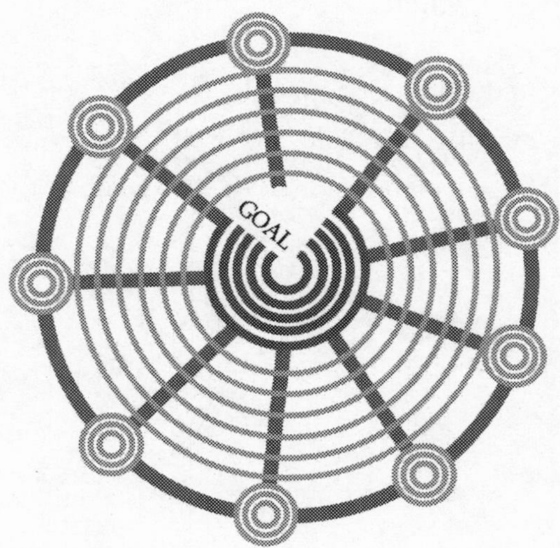

Figure 13: Community

Now, the hero's journey of every individual can begin, and in sharing the experiences, we weave the web of the community.

The students and alumni of the EBS University for Business and Law (EBS) are living a great example of a spiderweb with international threads. The university is a place where teachers and students are fully committed to their work. They follow through and strive to create something of value for the community. The price tag of the regular three-year-degree course is forty-two thousand euros. This is not the place for perpetual students. The degree is an investment. However, the students become part of an international community and a network of two hundred EBS partner universities spanning the globe, which they would have to establish on their own at regular schools. At the EBS, the network is part of the package, and a semester abroad is part of the curriculum.

Semiha Sandler knows that people calling the EBS an "elite school" do not mean it kindly. In Turkey, the birthplace of her parents, people think differently, she says. And the system is different, too. Some parents take out loans to send their children to the best schools in the country. A great education is the best investment in the future—with a lifelong dividend.

One of the projects of the EBS Institute for Transformation in Business and Society (INIT), where Semiha Sander serves as associate director of finance and administration, is the establishment of a continued education program for retired seniors who would like to found or work in a social business. Another project focuses on social innovations that can help with facing big challenges, such as fairness in education or the increase of widespread diseases. Field experience is an important part of an EBS education. People who get their degree here have spent considerable time in companies at home and abroad. This combination of practical work experience and time abroad is an excellent foundation for a successful career start, says Semiha. By the way, people who pass the EBS application process receive the financial aid they need through grants, school programs, and loans.

* * *

There is also a lot going on in another kind of community: the office. People in very different jobs use shared office space and become an "office community." It used to be that people sharing an office were in the same field, e.g., copywriters, graphic artists, and web designers, but now the industries are beginning to mingle.

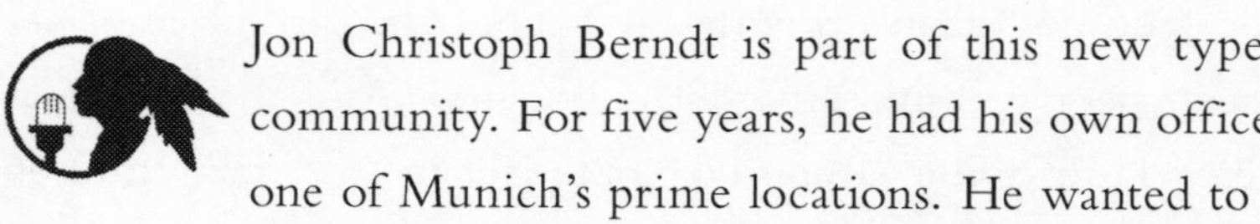

Jon Christoph Berndt is part of this new type of community. For five years, he had his own office in one of Munich's prime locations. He wanted to see what it was like to have his own office where he was boss and could do whatever he wanted. Bottom line: the location was not a success. And it was exhausting to be responsible for every cable and roll of toilet paper on top of being responsible for the people at the desks. For him, the new community in his shared office is a gift. Sharing does not mean having to do without; it is about gaining important advantages. It is a good give and take for all.

As I said in part 1, in the chapter "Growing Roots," today's communities are certainly a mix of virtual and face-to-face contacts.

One thing we tend to forget in this era of the digital natives is the archaic concept of holding council—of sitting by the fire and talking to each other. Council is something we have known from the very beginning of days, something that unites us. Although modern technology offers fantastic opportunities for global networking, we shouldn't forget personal human contact and conversations face-to-face.

For Native Americans, council was an essential part of their community. In council, they established relationships that were the foundation of their daily life. Council creates connections, empathy, teamwork, and trust.

> "The quality of our work in this world is determined by the quality of our relationships."
>
> –Gigi Coyle and Marlow Hotchkiss

I learned everything there is to know about council from Gigi Coyle. And I am still learning. For thirty years, Gigi has worked with individuals and groups from many different communities and cultures. She is a woman who connects worlds; she builds bridges in many international projects. She is also one of the authors of *The Way of Council* and *The Box: Remembering the Gift.* The following is inspired by council gatherings and intensive workshops Gigi taught with Marlow Hotchkiss, her colleague of many years, and by the workshop materials.

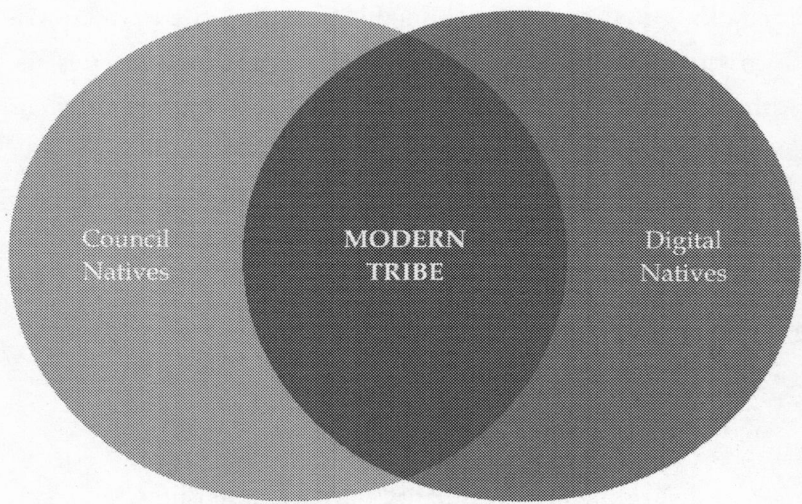

Figure 14: The Modern Tribe

How Does Council Work?

Council is a simple meeting in a circle (no laptops or cell phones). There is a council leader; ideally, there are two leaders, a man and a woman, if the group consists of both genders. The wisdom and healing, the insights and decisions in this circle are always based on the contributions of all members.

First, the topic is put before the group. It can be a question the team is dealing with or a current topic.

A talking staff, like the one The Chief uses, facilitates clear communication. In our world, it can be a computer mouse or a small ball—a small item important to the team or a little piece of nature that inspires or touches the group in some way.

For one form of council, one person takes the staff from the center of the circle and begins to speak. When he is finished, he hands the staff clockwise to the next person until the staff comes back to him and can be placed in the center of the circle again. The only person who speaks is the one holding the staff. Everybody else listens.

There is no right or wrong in council. It is about honest communication. There are a few simple guidelines:

- Speak from the heart.
- Listen with your heart.
- Be spontaneous. Don't think too much about the things that need to be said.
- Be brief. Practice finding the essence of the things you want to say.
- Try to find words for the things that serve you and/or the circle—and the world, as well—best.
- Personal things shared in this circle stay in the circle.

Council always reveals the truth. The circle develops its own dynamic. It is helpful if the council leader has some experience with this kind of work.

How Can We Use a Council?

A council can be used for many different purposes: to discover the soul of the group, to find a vision or resolve a conflict. Councils can be used for brainstorming and team building, for decisions and taking stock of the status quo to see where the participants stand. Storytelling can also be done in council, because it honors every individual and creates space for diversity instead of standardizing and ignoring things. You can hold council at the end of a project to reflect, evaluate, and determine the next steps.

Example of a Story Council

Friday is the day for stories in the department. The team meets at a certain time, and everybody gets a chance to tell about the experiences and special moments of his or her week. The first round is reserved for sharing the stories; in the second round, people can offer feedback and praise for the stories.

A learning council has four talking staff rounds. A learning council at the end of a project could be like this:

> Round 1: What happened? What ends today?
> Round 2: What are your thoughts and feelings at the end of this project?
> Round 3: What did you learn?
> Round 4: How does this experience enrich your life?

More councils, fewer meetings—that is the essence of this chapter. Let's not talk more; let's talk in a different way. Let's talk like people instead of machines. Let's weave a web between us and all other parties involved: our company, our customers, our partners, and the value that our product has for the world.

Something for your medicine bag: What does *community* mean to you? What are your communities in your professional and personal life? Find symbols for them and put them in your medicine bag.

Results of your medicine walk, with the subject "My Community":

CHAPTER 16

Elderhood: How to Cherish and Pass On Experience

Retirement party. Three older colleagues on the team are retiring. Sipping champagne, people say things like: "You are so lucky; you made it!" and "I'm green with envy;" and "When do you leave for the Bahamas?"

Two of the three look happy, relieved that this phase of their lives is over. Their faces show the demands of their work life.

"What are you looking forward to the most?" The Chief asks each of them.

The first man says, "My garden! My wife and I have been dreaming about having our own Tuscan garden for years. When I leave today, I'll go straight to the garden store."

The second man says, "My grandchildren. When my children were little, I was away so much that I missed out on a lot of things. I'll make up for that with my grandkids now."

The third man doesn't say anything. He has no wife, no children or grandchildren. Where will his journey take him? He doesn't know. He lifts his glass with a slightly trembling hand. The Chief looks at him with great warmth and kindness.

"Would you like to come here for a few hours every week and share your knowledge with us?" he asks quietly, so that the others don't hear him.

The man looks surprised. Then he relaxes. His hand stops trembling, and something lights up his eyes as he says, "Yes, I would like that very much."

* * *

Native Americans have great respect for the life experience of older people. Many tribes had a council of elders, consisting of old, wise men, brave warriors, and respected women. The council determined when the time was right for a hunt and whether or not the tribe should go on the warpath. The council organized the work of all family members, even the women and children, who were assigned fields, crops, and seasonal tasks.

The elder council was even more important than the chief. It made the decisions, which the chief passed on. This is an important point, because no Native American wielded absolute power over the tribe. The elder council ruled the village or camp and made most decisions.

It was common for younger people to ask their elders for advice. For Native Americans, such conversations were a regular part of the life of Native Americans. Topics included the land, seasonal changes, habits of the animals, and locations of useful plants. The knowledge of the elders was important for the community, for the survival of the entire tribe. Therefore, old people were revered.

What Did Old and Young People Talk About?

Most stories of the elders had several purposes. The younger generations learned how to hunt, travel, and survive by taking the experiences of the past into the future. Grandparents introduced their grandchildren to the traditions of the tribe. Legends, fairy tales, and creation myths were passed on this way, as well as the dances and songs of the tribe.

Young people respected the elders. It was rude to even speak to an older person without being addressed by them first.

Central and North American tribes were organized into clans; some still are. The chief of the clan and the elder council handle all issues of the village community.

In many tribes, particularly among Plains Indians, old and sick people were left behind on walks to die alone. It was not the community who wanted to get rid of them; the old people chose the time of their death, independently and of sound mind. Their physical and mental condition guided them in their decision. Indigenous people sensed when it was time to go to the "happy hunting ground," as Native Americans call the afterlife.

How Can We Conserve and Pass On the Experience of Our Elders Today?

In most companies, the retirement of longstanding employees means a great loss of knowledge. There are some attempts to create an electronic archive of this knowledge by storing it in CMS systems and knowledge databases. In most cases, these attempts create nothing but a data graveyard. A much better approach is to recognize that storytelling can be a way to pass on the knowledge of the elders in a way that keeps it useful for the company. We will discuss the subject of storytelling in more depth later on.

Another good way to cherish the wisdom of the elders is to keep them in the company in a mentor program, in which every young manager receives support from an elder.

The best solution seems to be a little bit of everything: storing some knowledge in a digital archive, passing on some knowledge as stories, and, last but certainly not least, learning from the way the elders did things.

In one of our conversations, Meredith Little, the founder of the School of Lost Borders, touched on a very interesting aspect. If the elders listen to the young people instead of telling them what to do, if they listen instead of judging and criticizing, the young people will be more willing to listen to them. Both parties create a natural mentor relationship at eye level, based on deep communication, honest sharing, and true cooperation. The elders should bear a few basic requirements in mind:

- Listen.
- Put your own story and judgments aside for a while.
- Do not try to "fix" things or play therapist to the younger person.
- Know your own work so well that you know your story and can use it as support.
- Be there for the other person.

- Know your own limitations and shadows.
- Be confident, so that your own ego is not an issue.

This is not a comprehensive list. It is meant as a starting point as your own thoughts and relationships grow.

What Could Be Appropriate Rituals in This Situation?

Not all elders are the same. Some people retire still bitter about the promotion they did not get; some have a hard time accepting the end of their professional life. Mentoring should involve those retirees who are satisfied with their own situation. They know where they stand and look back on their achievements with pride. They are willing to share their knowledge and experiences.

Apart from mentoring, there is an advanced council technique, the so-called "fishbowl of the generations."

A small circle sits at the center, the elders. They share stories using the talking staff. An outer circle of observers, the younger generation, listens attentively and may comment when the elders have finished their conversation. Taking part and witnessing the things that are important to the other generation promotes mutual understanding. Naturally, the fishbowl works the other way around, too: the younger people sit in the small circle, and the elders observe.

Another method is storytelling. The elders tell the younger generation about things, such as the greatest successes of their careers: What motivated me? What did I learn from it? But also: What was my biggest disappointment, and what did I learn from it? This is a kind of "fireside chat" between the elders and the next generation.

VAUDE follows another, very practical approach:

New employees are assigned a mentor. Twice a year, the company hosts an event called "Get the Spirit." It is about values, leadership, and positioning. The new employees receive the information they need and can turn to their personal mentor to teach them how the system works.

The German Association for the Club of Rome uses elderhood in a very successful way: for projects and initiatives for the younger generation, the goal is determined together, and everybody works toward it. The common goal, the common vision, brings people together. They understand each other better and even end up with a concrete result to show for it.

How Could We Establish an Elder Council in a Modern Company?

I find it fascinating that so many current studies talk about Generations X and Y. Elders are not even a subject for discussion anymore. It seems as if people sixty-plus years old are invisible and without value.

As I read McKinsey and others who study the young-manager generation, I cannot find anything about elders either.

The famous Generation X consists of people born after 1970. They strive for wealth and status symbols. Generation Y, the so-called "Millennials," are people born after 1985. They strive for self-determination, fulfillment, and work-life balance.

It is no secret that there is some tension between Generations X and Y and older people. The Millennials say that they are uncomfortable when working with older people. Thirty-eight percent say that the senior management does not fit in with the younger employees, and 34 percent believe that their personal drive scares the other generation. (Source: PWC Managing Tomorrow's People)

It seems to me that we are not dealing with a workplace problem here, but with a problem in our society.

A corporate elder council would be a great thing. And in a way, it already exists, as the supervisory board of a corporation. However, the board members are often not elders, but rather people who are respected for their political or societal status and supposed to give the company more prestige.

When does a person become a wise elder? And more importantly: Who says? I think it only makes sense if the elders are appointed by the employees. It would be a different kind of workers' council. The elders could appoint the next elders. With their office, they take on the responsibility for the fate of the company and for training the younger employees. And they keep the rituals alive.

I was fortunate enough to know a true elder. He passed away in the summer of 2012. He was a senior manager at a major Swiss company, one of my clients. We worked together for years, and he always kept the company politics away from me, so that I was able to do my work. In small steps, he introduced me into the company (and its groups and factions) and all important decision makers. At the time, I was not aware how much he protected me.

When he died unexpectedly, I realized how much of a buffer he had been. Without him, I was twisting in the wind.

I am very grateful for our time together. It gave me many opportunities to grow and mature. And it was a great example of what a corporate elder can and should be, how being a role model really works.

A company elder keeps politics away so that talents and skills can unfold. An elder has no interest in company politics, because he doesn't have to worry about his profile anymore. He is a human shield protecting developing talents and personalities.

When he died, I became a "yelder" (younger elder) in the company. Since then, I have seen how difficult things are for his successor, how the team reacts to him and the new situation, and how a new dynamic is emerging bit by bit.

Let's recap: Generation Y needs different leadership than Generation X. That means even Generation X gets a chance to learn and do a "chief crash course." And both generations need the support of elders, who envelop them in the warm protection of their knowledge and experience.

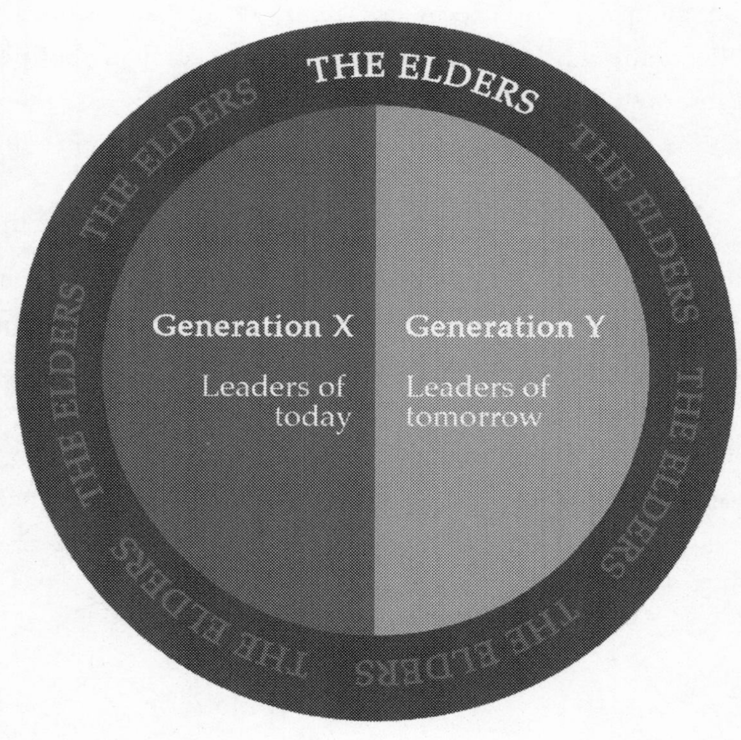

Figure 15: Generations X and Y and the elders.

Who Would Be a Good Example of a Chief or Elder Today?

I don't need to think much about the answer to this question: Claus Hipp.

The Chief and Claus Hipp have a lot in common: The Chief is dressed in traditional buckskin garments, while Claus Hipp wears a traditional loden suit. This man does not just stand for tradition, he lives it. His family has a motto he learned from his grandfather: "Do the right thing, fear God, and look everybody in the eye."

He lives his faith quite openly and is the one who unlocks the church doors early in the morning. His face says, "I am curious about life." Where other people his age or even younger look old and exhausted, he still has a twinkle in his eye. In his career as an entrepreneur, he is said to be a pioneer of organic agriculture and ethical corporate leadership. To me, he is much, much more; he is the embodiment of the word *righteous*. And he has remained humble despite his success. He knows that he cannot take his acquired wealth with him when he leaves this life one day.

I think it is very interesting when he says that we, as entrepreneurs, need to keep an eye on the big picture and on creation—but that creation needs to serve us, too. Environmental concerns, for instance, should not limit us in our thinking and action. We need to create jobs *and* be good stewards of the environment and all wildlife. Sustainability without exploitation. Everybody takes just what he needs and takes care not to damage the next generation.

He compares the role of the chief with the conductor of an orchestra. The conductor needs to know what he wants and how the piece should be played, but he does not have to play the violin better than the concertmaster. In his company, there is a sustainability officer who reports directly to management and checks that the company's business decisions are useful in the long term without damaging the next generation.

Claus Hipp's children are lucky: they saw their father's enthusiasm for the company from an early age and learned about his strong, clear values, which were: tradition. Sustainability. Healthy growth that goes easy on the employees and the company's resources. Thoughts and actions that go far beyond one's own interests. Charity and help for the poor, which Claus Hipp keeps out of the media. And the inner fire burning for a product that has nurtured generations of children, ensuring their healthy growth.

I meet a Hipp employee at a store. Swooning, she tells me that she loves two men in her life: God and Claus Hipp.

He laughs when I tell him about this. He is a modest man. A humble man who follows the natural cycle of give and take, surrounded and supported by a strong family and a strong team of people, some of whom he knew as babies. A man who cares for everybody.

Something for your medicine bag: Which object signifies living wisdom for you? In which parts of your life do you already have the status of an advisor and are able to support others, because you have already made that journey—or at least parts of it? Who are your role models, the elders you look up to?

Results of your medicine walk, with the subject "Elders":

CHAPTER 17

Rituals: Creating Common Ground

A sign has been posted on the coffeemaker that says: "Effective immediately, coffee and tea consumption during work hours is prohibited. Please also refrain from gathering in groups of more than one person in the kitchen and cafeteria. Smoking is strictly prohibited everywhere on company premises. Management."

The departments are up in arms. No more coffee breaks? No more cigarette breaks? Not even a quick chat with a colleague? Are they out of their minds upstairs? The employees talk passionately about the outrageous decision and its possible motives. One would think they were just robbed of their greatest treasure. However, they don't talk long, because they are no longer allowed to gather in groups. After a few minutes, everybody goes on his or her own way—alone, angry, and frustrated. Stunned. Productivity today? Zero.

* * *

For many of us, a cup of coffee or tea in the morning with a chat in the kitchen or out in the hallway has become a ritual. It is simply part of our workday. What other rituals do we have in our everyday business life? Not many, if you look at it closely. Some companies have a casual Friday. But is that really a ritual or just an occasion to exchange information: Where are we? What happened? What was successful? Where do we have to go?

People need rituals. Rituals give our lives support and structure. Having dinner with the family, brushing your teeth in the morning and at night, going to church on Sunday.

My team and I went out to dinner today. We celebrated and said our good-byes, because Brigitte is going to Nepal for four weeks. It is important to us to give those who have the courage to go on a journey—on vacation or for a project—an appropriate send-off. We celebrate their courage and send them on their journey with our best wishes.

Which Rituals Are Appropriate for Our Time and Can Be Easily Integrated into Our Work Life?

The Talking Staff

The talking staff, as we have seen already, is used whenever the group comes together. Either the group selects their own staff, or it can be something that has been used for generations (Native Americans sometimes use a flute). On the vision quests, where I served as a guide, we built the talking staff together: everybody hangs an object of their choice on a piece of wood. This creates a common base and a tool that the entire group can accept. In my work as an IT consultant, I often use modern objects, such as a computer mouse. Anything that works for this group can be used. The talking staff lends security because we can hold onto it. And it gives confidence in explaining your own point of view, because it works as a silent ally. At the same time, it stands for an important rule: only the person holding the staff speaks.

The use of such a tool promotes a culture of communication and discipline, of choosing your words carefully and of active listening. Each point of view is important. Everybody may finish his or her thoughts. Everyone is heard.

A talking staff can also be equipped with symbols for the quarterly goals. When the group meets to exchange ideas, the staff reminds them of their starting point and of their goal, thus strengthening the team spirit.

The Council

The tradition of sitting around the campfire is as old as the world. Sitting in a circle around the fire leads to an authentic exchange of ideas. People speak and listen from the heart. At the campfire, the fate of the tribe was decided, stories were shared, and the elders met.

The technique of council—we talked about it in the chapter "Common Sense"—is being revived today all over the world, especially in working with groups, families, and couples. In the business world, council is rarely used, even though it is an incomparable asset that forges true team spirit.

While we may not be able to light a fire in a conference room, we can still mark the center of the circle, perhaps by placing the talking staff in the center at the beginning and at the end of the conversation.

And, of course, the council cannot replace regular meetings with agendas and presentations. A council complements these exchanges, offering its own strengths and benefits.

A council has a few very simple rules. Some of them we discussed in the chapter "Common Sense." The following rules focus on the council's function as a ritual:

- We sit in a circle.
- We use the talking staff.
- The person holding the staff speaks.
- Everybody else listens attentively.
- Be in the moment.
- Speak from the heart.
- All in the circle meet at eye-level.
- Try to understand instead of attacking.
- Look for the collective truth, not just your own.
- Listen to the things said and not said between the lines.
- Formulate questions instead of justifications.
- The team has top priority, not your own achievements.
- Be honest and don't try to be right at all cost.
- Trust, don't doubt.
- There is a council leader.
- The council has a clear beginning and end.

One clearly marked ending of a council session could be that everybody stands up and applauds. Each group can find their own finishing ritual.

A council is not appropriate for the following situations or purposes:

- Business meetings with PowerPoint
- Discussions
- General exchange of information
- Q & A sessions

For these situations, there are two tools that can be used to create structure and the format of a ritual.

The Meeting Bell

Sometimes, things go awry and discussions become endless or veer off topic. A bell in the conference room (like the one at some hotel reception desks) can be used to give a signal to pause for a moment in these situations. When the bell rings, everybody stops talking and takes a few deep breaths before resuming the conversation and returning to the matter at hand. At the start of the meeting, one person is designated to ring the bell, if necessary.

Taking a deep breath is generally a good idea when it comes to resolving a gridlocked discussion. So here is another important tool.

The Pause for Breath

Sometimes we answer too quickly. Without taking the time to understand the position of the other person, the words just slip out of my mouth. The technique of the pause for breath can help.

Take four deep breaths before answering. The answers tend to be more constructive. For Native Americans, a pause before speaking is normal. It is a sign of respect for my conversation partner. I give his words time to reach not just my ears, but also my heart.

Other rituals in the modern business world are:

The Medicine Bag

We already talked in depth about the medicine bag in part 1 of this book. In terms of rituals, I would like to add that it is a great sign of appreciation for all employees if they receive something for their medicine bags at the end of a successful year. This serves as a symbol for the individual's personal growth.

Burden Basket

Native American women had a basket they used to gather wood, herbs, fruit, and other food. When the woman was at home, the basket hung at the entrance to her teepee and became the burden basket. For Native Americans, it was considered rude if a visitor brought his own worries and problems into the sacred space of another. Before entering the teepee, he symbolically placed everything that was a burden to him in the basket. There was a rule that a person should never carry more worries than he could physically carry in the basket. This basket reminds us that we need to work on our own challenges in order to reduce our burden. If we need to resolve our own issues, we go to the elders or to the medicine man or woman and have a conversation with them.

I often wonder what would happen in corporate meetings if everybody laid down their own problems at the door to the conference room. We would then enter a neutral space that would offer a wealth of new possibilities.

In part 1, we already discussed the significance of the warbonnet and the rites of passage. Let me encourage you again to create your symbolic warbonnet that reminds you of your achievements and victories. And we should celebrate and witness the transitions in the work life of every individual: from trainee to team member, from team member to manager, from manager to elder, from elder to retiree.

I would like to introduce one last ritual: the giveaway ceremony.

The Giveaway Ceremony

This was a ceremony in which the members of the tribe met to give each other valuable personal objects. The tradition was to give from the heart and with humility. People believed in giving without the expectation of receiving something in return, in personal and community growth through sharing convictions, possessions, and stories. Wealth was measured by the selflessness with which talents were shared. Only people who knew how to give, truly and generously, were qualified to become leaders.

And the Native Americans even went a step further: they believed that people who did not share their talents and knowledge would lose their "medicine" (their potential and gifts).

This is an interesting idea, considering our constant fear of having our ideas stolen from us and the phenomenon of "mobbing."

It is time to build trust in our teams and in our company. And we need to give from the heart without expecting an immediate promotion or raise in return.

Something for your medicine bag: Which rituals are important to you? Which rituals do you remember from your childhood? Which of them could you integrate into your life today? Find a symbol for your favorite ritual that gives you strength and comfort, keeps you healthy, or makes you laugh.

Results of your medicine walk, with the subject "Rituals":

CHAPTER 18

Storytelling: How Knowledge Is Kept Alive and Connects Us

The conference room is buzzing. It's official now: the company was acquired by a big competitor. The Chief is the only silent person in the room. Julia is sitting next to him.

"Aren't you happy?" she asks. "This is a great success for all of us!"

The Chief stares into the distance and tells a legend of the Ute:

"On a bison hunt, a porcupine came to a wide river. A bison herd grazed peacefully along the bank.

'Carry me over,' said the porcupine.

'Who, me?' asked the first bison grazing nearby.

'No,' said the picky porcupine and called out again. He rejected all offers until the last bison came. He was the biggest and strongest animal in the herd.

'Climb on my back,' the bison said.

'No,' answered the porcupine. 'I'd fall into the water.'

'Then sit between my horns.'

'No,' came the answer. 'I might slide off!'

'Then I'll carry you in my belly to the other side.'

'All right,' said the porcupine and allowed himself to be swallowed by the bison.

'Where are we?' asked the porcupine after a while.

'In the middle of the river,' answered the bison. As he climbed out of the water, he said, 'Now we are there.'

'Wait,' the porcupine called out of the bison's mouth. 'Walk a little further.'

After a few steps, the bison stopped and said, 'Come out now!'

The porcupine slapped his great, big tail against the bison's heart. The bison collapsed and died."

The Chief pauses and then says, "This story shows that this kind of merger can only be successful if it is clear how we deal with our joint powers. Otherwise, we might suffer losses that may never have been intended—and harm innocent people.

"The question is: Were we scared to cross the river as a small company and went to hunt for a strong partner? Or did we want to join forces with our new partner to reach the other side faster?

"Something always has to die in a merger. What will it be for us? Will we be able to keep our culture? Will they ask us?"

* * *

The poet Muriel Rukeyser gets to the heart of the matter, saying: "The Universe is made of stories, not atoms." Stories are the basic material of our communities and our culture. We grow up with (bedtime) stories; we tell stories as teenagers and later as adults to our colleagues and friends. Peoples and tribes who embrace a less high-tech culture pass on their knowledge in stories instead of bits and bytes that are stored in never-ending data graveyards.

The Celts insisted that only poets could become teachers. Why? The American priest and theologian Matthew Fox has an interesting answer: Because knowledge that has not gone through the heart is dangerous. It could lack wisdom. He asks: What would happen if our education system insisted on having poets, storytellers, and artists as teachers? Which transformations would occur?

In Native American cultures, legends, cultural wealth, old knowledge, and current events were passed on by a storyteller. The storyteller traveled from tribe to tribe, passing along the traditions not just to his own people, but to people in the entire region. It was an important job. Moreover, storytelling was the way of communicating news—such as births and deaths. One could say that storytellers were the first daily newspapers and tabloid magazines.

Naturally, stories were also a part of every family and tribe. There were often two storytellers, one male, one female. The man passed on the legends of the warriors, and the woman told the myths and stories of healing powers and feminine skills.

The storyteller also belonged to the Circle of Elders. He was an elder who brought his own wisdom, the experiences of his own life, and the wisdom of the crowds out into the world.

There were different stories of varying depth. Some stories were told only to at the council of elders, while others were meant for the entire tribe. They all had one thing in common: they were about growth and expansion. The attentive listeners always learned something about themselves, found a piece of their own human puzzle and put it in its place, thus walking a step farther on their paths.

Native Americans believed that true support of the growth of each individual can only be given if each member of the tribe is allowed to understand and process things at his own pace. So, the same stories were told again and again from different angles to offer all listeners a chance to find their own meaning in the story. Instead of rushing people in their learning process, they were allowed to take in the new information in their own good time.

Stories were told in a circle—of course. Children were placed at eye-level with the storyteller. Most of the time, a bright fire was the center of the circle. People took their time; they did not tell their stories in passing. The setting had to be right. And their hearts were in it: they spoke and listened from the heart. This aspect cannot be stressed enough. The immediate connection created true fellowship and the greatest possible personal growth.

Winter was the time for stories. People had to spend more time in their teepees, because nature and all living things had withdrawn to rest. I wonder what our business world would be like if we made more time for stories in winter.

How Can We Frame Our Corporate Knowledge in a Story to Make It Immortal?

I would like to show you three different ways: telling stories to create a tribe, stories about a generation change. And stories at the end of a life.

The first example comes from my own work life.

Creating a Tribe with Stories: Piedmont 2012

Every year, our team takes a trip to work on the strategy for the coming year. In 2012, we traveled to the Piedmont region in Italy. Under the heading of "Listen – Mirror – Strengthen," each of us had twenty minutes to tell our story of the past year—about the company, projects, people, our work, our personal life … everything was of equal importance.

As the chief, I summarized the stories in order to mirror them. This gave me an opportunity to convey my appreciation and praise at a much deeper level. Following my mirroring, the other people in the circle were invited to support the storyteller with their feedback. This form of storytelling creates a web of appreciation and deep, honest communication that I have never seen before in my business life. *We moved from team to tribe.*

We turned our Piedmont 2012 experience into a booklet that we sent to our clients and partners as a Christmas present to share our experience with them. Documenting our story is not quite part of the tradition of storytelling, but it gives us the opportunity to capture the essence of the stories and share them with people who are not near us and cannot sit with us in the circle. Thus, the connectedness and message of the circle can reach far beyond the event. On the first page of our booklet, we printed our creed for the coming year: "If you want to travel fast, go alone. If you want to travel far, go with others."

Marking a Generation Change with Stories

A friend of mine, who is currently helping a company with its change of generations, told me this story:

The father and founder of the company wants to pass on the reigns to his two children. This kind of transition is a difficult thing. Storytelling offers the father an opportunity to condense and relate the things that were important to him in the course of his professional life. Now, the two generations and other leaders have regular meetings in which the father tells stories from his career, about things that had a great impact on him and the company. The process is going to take a whole year—and it is not just about sharing the traditions, successes, and failures, but also about establishing a new culture of storytelling and listening in the company.

Stories About the End of a Life

In 2012, a senior manager of one of my clients died unexpectedly. His sudden death was a shock for all employees. The man had been part of the company for twenty years, and his death left a huge hole. Those who had been by his side for a long time had a hard time finding their way back into their everyday lives. It was frightening to see how day-to-day business operations continued (had to continue), while the employees were suffering in silence.

I met with the management team to find a solution for a dignified and respectful ritual marking the end of everybody's time with this man. We came up with the following: on a late-summer afternoon, the team met at a small pond in a nature sanctuary. Almost thirty people gathered. A moderator began the conversation. Standing in a circle, we all told brief stories about how this man touched our lives. In the second round, we offered our wishes for the journey of the deceased.

With our stories, we honored the deceased and also reminded ourselves as a group of the great gift of having been able to spend so much time together. Growing together. Even failing together. There were tears in the circle; people expressed their grief. Everybody was allowed to show his or her feelings in any way.

As humans, we are joyful, we grieve, we laugh, and we cry. In a group, these moments attain even more significance. It is said that a sorrow shared is a sorrow halved. And shared joy is joy doubled. Our afternoon by the pond kept the memory of the deceased alive in us.

Stories About the Beauty in All Things: Gaby Just (JUST PURE)

I met Gaby Just at a café in Munich in January of 2013. It was a very special interview. We talked as if we had known each other for ages. With some people, you experience the feeling of the familiarity of old friends, even though you just met for the first time. It was that way with Gaby Just. Gaby is a beautiful woman. She and her husband live on a secluded farm in the Allgäu Alps. She chose their home to be one with nature—just as her products are one with nature. This direct connection is important to her.

Homemade jam gave her the idea of the moon phases. All her jars of homemade jam spoiled overnight. A neighbor told her: "You need to make your preserves with the moon!" On this day, Gaby conceived her special production process based on anthroposophical principles—the "lunar phases" concept.

Gaby Just is a woman who lives the principle of "the right time"—not just in terms of the moon, but in all parts of her life. A few years ago, she bought an old house in a village on the island of Majorca. A very old, decrepit house. Gaby Just began her career as an interior decorator. She was not scared of the decay around her; she was motivated! She bought the house for three thousand pesetas—about fifteen dollars in today's money—and rebuilt it step by step. The house, which used to belong to the village prostitute, who had offered her services in a kind of barter system, became the most beautiful house in the village. People would stop and admire the house. Laughing, Gaby Just says that she liked the positive energy of the house. She likes to think that the former occupant made people happy in it.

For Gaby Just, beauty is not a matter or appearance or age. She believes that it is important to have a vision as you age, and an answer to the question: What will give me joy when I am old?

What can we learn from Gaby's story?

- Look beneath the surface.
- Don't be prejudiced.
- Look for beauty even among ruins.
- Have faith. Neither Gaby nor the real estate agent were sure that the down payment of fifteen dollars would ensure that both parties would stick to the agreement.
- Beauty is timeless.

Of Wheels and Spokes: My Own Story

While I am writing this, I am reminded of a story from my own life. It is about the wheel of life, which is why I want to tell it to you.

You could say that I am an expert in wheels. When I was twelve years old, I worked in a bicycle shop. The first thing they taught me was how to build wheels. Nobody liked this job, because it required incredible patience. I agreed. At first, I hated this job with a passion. It took an entire day to build a wheel set. It sucked.

The easiest task was getting the spokes into the correct order. But the most important thing was the *tension* on every single spoke.

In order to build a wheel that will run smoothly, you do not just need patience; you need the right feeling for it. It is an art form. I spent ten years perfecting this art. Building wheels became my form of meditation. While my colleagues were using modern measuring tools to set the tension, I used my senses. I knew the sound a spoke made when it had the right tension. The wheel's vibration told me whether I had put on too much or too little tension. I knew that even the smallest adjustments made it necessary to turn the wheel a few times to see the impact of the change on the entire system. And I always remembered that many adjustments and turns are necessary until everything runs smoothly.

Eventually, I found it more interesting to repair broken wheels. With every repair came a person with a story, which he or she told me while I was changing spokes or rims. When I gave them the repaired wheel, it seemed sometimes as if something inside of them had gone back in its right place, too, as if there were a tiny bit of healing in the wheel of their life, while I was busy with a part of their bicycle. It might seem strange, but I think that my ability to listen, to sense things and feel them deeply, was born in those days, when I built and repaired hundreds of bicycle wheels. Today, I continue my work with the wheel, invisibly—with people and groups. The basics are still the same.

What can we learn from this story?

- Every person has a story.
- All experiences are valuable and shape our personality.
- Sometimes, it takes a while to make sense of your experiences.

* * *

Whatever stories we may tell each other, let's tell them! In today's fast-paced, high-tech world, there is something we lose all too often: high-touch. Being touched. Being moved deep within. And feeling the connection with other people that these things create. Where we have stories, we are one—whether we come from America or Europe, from the Middle East, Asia, or Africa. The echo such stories create within us is as old as the birth of the continents. It goes straight to our hearts. Stories connect us to our hearts, our bodies, our fellow man, and our country.

Native American author and poet Paula Gunn Allen says in her book *The Sacred Hoop*: "Illness is a result of separation from the ancient unity of person, ceremony, and land, and healing is a result of recognition of this unity.... Perhaps we can best characterize this relation by saying that the stories are the communication device of the land and the people. Through the stories, the ceremony, the gap between isolate human being and lonely landscape is closed." (Gunn Allen,1992,119)

* * *

In my Piedmont story, I talked about mirroring. But before a story can be mirrored, before we can learn how to use this tool, we need to learn to appreciate stories and to listen. Here, I would like to give you some tips that will help you with your appreciation of stories, so that you can take the first steps toward mirroring.

Honoring Stories

Creating the Right Setting

1. A deep story is not told quickly, in passing. Take time and make room. All phones are switched off.
2. Do not interrupt the storyteller. Let him finish his story. Out of respect for the story, you should pause for a moment. Then it is your time to talk.
3. Even if you know the story, try listening to it as if you were hearing it for the very first time.
4. It is a gift to witness a story. It makes us open ourselves to one another. We can reward the storyteller by listening closely. By listening from the heart.

Honoring the Story as a Mirror

1. Imagine that you look into your bathroom mirror in the morning. What you say to the storyteller should be a reflection of what you heard. After all, you don't tell your mirror image that it should have done everything differently. Smile at the reflection and say with all of your heart: "I like you. You are brave, wonderful, and unique."
2. Which parts of the story have touched you most? And what lies beneath? Is it courage, caring, kindness? Feel free to express that.
3. Your own story does not belong in your comments. This is about the storyteller's story!
4. A mirror is neutral and should be encouraging. It is not an exercise in growth or a therapy session.

Something for your medicine bag: Which symbol or object stands for your story? Look for the stories of your childhood, adolescence, and adulthood. Did you ever repair a bicycle wheel? Which seemingly unimportant experiences are now helping you in your job?

Results of your medicine walk, with the subject "Storytelling: My stories":

CHAPTER 19

Happiness: The Right Balance of Meaning and Material Things

The HR manager looks serious. His numbers are not good. Last year, too many people quit their jobs. Recruiting costs skyrocketed. The new people were not always the best and had to be replaced or shuffled into other jobs. The manager gives The Chief an expectant look.

"So, how do I keep the good people? I'm at my wits' end here!"

Instead of answering, The Chief asks, "Are your people happy?"

The HR guy raises his eyebrows. "Happy, happy … what does that even mean? We try to give everybody a nice workspace, reasonable hours, not too much overtime."

* * *

Unemployment is in decline. This should make us happy, but there is a flip side of the coin: current studies about people's job satisfaction make the smile freeze on our faces. Fewer and fewer people are happy in their jobs. An in-house survey at Deutsche Bahn showed that 70 percent of its employees are unhappy at work. A Gallup poll showed that nine out of ten employees are working while having mentally quit their jobs. Compared to the rest of Europe, Germany ranks in the lower middle in terms of job satisfaction, says the Duisburg Institute for Work, Skills, and Training (IAQ). Only people in Eastern Europe are unhappier than we are. What does that mean?

It means, quite simply, that we just work to make money. We tick off the hours and are relieved when the day is finally over. We work to pay for our mortgage, car, college for the kids … being happy with your job? It is an almost ridiculous notion.

It is, however, exactly what a good chief wants. We need to be in the position that suits us, that we find fulfilling and challenging. The chief knows that a bad mood makes for bad work. A warrior who just shuffles off after the bison heard without any real motivation or drive will come home empty-handed.

But where is the company that has enough money to take care of the happiness and potential of the employees? We need sales, strategies, cost-cutting, being cheaper, having a competitive edge, remaining attractive to our customers and shareholders. Everything else is just useless nonsense. Too bad that this nonsense keeps coming up in more and more surveys and can no longer be ignored.

What can a company do to achieve its goals and "produce" happy employees at the same time? How does a chief make his whole tribe happy *and* have a successful hunt?

Google wondered about that. Not quite voluntarily, but because the company had a huge problem a few years ago. A conspicuous number of women who had just given birth quit their jobs, as Fahrrad Manjoo writes in his Slate Magazine Article: *The Happiness Machine.*

Now, Google is a company that already offers pretty good quality of work life. There is a reason why *Fortune* magazine named it "best employer" (Microsoft ranked seventy-fifth; Apple, Amazon, and Facebook were not even on the list). Google employees get free gourmet food, have a dry-cleaning service at the Googleplex and can use Wi-Fi commuter shuttles. Moreover, the management even considered the perfect size and shape of the cafeteria tables and the best length (or shortness) of the daily lunch lines.

Google found an elegant solution for their "new-mother problem." If you have a child, you are offered five months of paid maternity leave. You can even split those five months. A new mom can come back to work after couple of weeks or months and take the rest of her leave later, when the child is a little older.

Why on earth is Google doing this? It costs money!

Sure it does. But it costs much more money to have all those women leave and then have to go through the expensive, time-consuming recruitment process. They know this.

Now they have created a win-win situation: the women are happy, and the company is, too.

This is just one example of how companies can make their employees happy. Other problems affect men and women equally, such as when parents get older, need surgery, or just need to have a caregiver for a while. There are some flexible model programs, offered by companies that care about their employees and their happiness.

Fact is: money alone does not buy happiness. Happiness is a complex structure that looks very different for each person. And happiness is a matter of age. What makes a fifty-year-old, or someone reaching retirement age, happy is not the same thing that makes Generations X and Y—or the "digital cowboys," as Prof. Mark Müller-Eberstein calls them in his eponymous book—happy. Young people want to be challenged. They are happy when they can work independently, with flexibility of time and space, when they can work from home or from their smartphone—and if all business processes are fully transparent.

They all have one thing in common, though: they want to be a part of the company's developments and decisions.

> "Only if I share in the path of its development I can say yes to the company I work for."
>
> –Theo Knaus

Sounds like making all these people happy is a lifetime task. And maybe it is. But maybe it is easier than we think. Maybe it is about asking one fundamental question.

Who Are My People?

Not everybody—that much is obvious. Not everybody fits into our company, just like not every single person in the world wants our products and services—even if we would like it to be that way. We have certain target groups who want and need our products and services. And there are certain types of people who fit into our company. We need to give both groups the chance to find out for themselves. Employees who fit in need to feel that every day. And employees who do not fit in need to be able to recognize that, too, and act accordingly. For many people, their job pays the rent. But there have always been those people who see their job as a fulfilling part of their lives—their life's work. And the number of those kinds of people is growing.

Who are my people? What makes them stand out? What do they feel? How do they live? And with whom? How do they find happiness in their relationships? What are their challenges? How can I, as their employer, give them the best support so that they can handle all demands of their workday calmly and joyfully? How do I manage to make this great orchestra—to use Claus Hipp's beautiful image—of different personalities and cultures play in harmony? And keep them all healthy?

Are phenomena such as burnout a result of our fast-paced business world? Ute Küffner asked that question more than once. We always want more, always pick up speed—and there is nothing that nurtures us. Nobody asks "Why?" Things we can influence are meaningful to us. But when someone says, "Just do it, and don't worry about what happens afterwards," we do not find meaning in that. The demands are piling up—and our soul gets sick. We cannot trick or fake the things we need to live well. There is something deeper at work here. The needs of our soul always come to light.

VAUDE takes great care of its employees' needs. The company offers all kinds of work programs: full-time, part-time, home office, part home office … people stay healthy with in-house yoga and massages as well as climbing and biking workshops. People who want to switch from car to bike can use an eBike from the eBike pool. And there are measures in place to reduce stress. People are not supposed to answer e-mails or make business calls on weekends.

Antje von Dewitz hopes that her grandchildren will say about her: "She did something." I think she is well on her way, indoors and outdoors.

* * *

If you haven't taken a medicine walk yet, now is the time. Look forward to it, and enjoy your curiosity about the answers that nature has for your questions: Who are my people? How do I make them happy? And who am I? What makes me happy?

When Native Americans move, they don't even take a hundred things. We would probably fill the moving truck with a few thousand. What do we really need? And could it be a luxury to be able to afford not to need everything? Perhaps you would like to take this thought with you on your medicine walk.

Something for your medicine bag: Hopefully, your medicine bag is now filled with things that strengthen you and remind you of the important things. Now, select an object that stands for your happiness.

Take your medicine bag with you to important meetings. Keep filling it with symbols that stand for your personal path. It is fun to look at your things from time to time. What is in my medicine bag? Which things want to stay? Which want to take their leave? Which symbol wants to be gifted to a dear colleague or friend (possibly in a give-away ceremony)? Use the power of your personal medicine bag; use it as a reflection of your unique nature and the inner and outer path you have walked in your life so far. Congratulations!

Results of your medicine walk, with the subject "Happiness":

CHAPTER 20

Planning for the Future: The Next Seven Generations

Felix Finkbeiner is fifteen years old and more mature than many adults I meet in my consultations. He is courageous. He is authentic. He is not yet blinded by a career and his life. And he grew up surrounded by true elders.

When Felix was five years old, his father took him to sustainability conferences. Today, he is one of the founders of the youth organization Plant-for-the-Planet. The goal of this organization is to plant a thousand billion trees by 2020 and to build the foundation for global climate justice. Trees are the only "machines" capable of binding the greenhouse gas carbon dioxide (CO_2), which is responsible for the climate crisis. Trees are the only way to slow down and eventually stop climate change, says Felix.

He never dreamed that the questions he asked as a nine-year-old in a fourth-grade presentation on climate change would be the beginning of a global movement. He never expected to shake hands with Kofi Annan and speak before the United Nations, give interviews all over the world, or become a UN youth ambassador for climate justice in order to work for a clean future for the children of the world. And he never knew that planting trees would be such an emotional and symbolic act. Everybody can plant trees, young and old, rich and poor, sick and healthy, people of any color … Felix calls it the "world family." If we, as a world family, stick together and work together, we can solve all our problems—not just climate change.

Because I Live Longer Than You is a documentary by Henriette Bornkamm and Cal-A. Fechner about Felix and the work he does with children and teenagers all over the world. His path begins where adults have been unable to find a solution for decades—where we are too lazy, too indifferent, to ignorant, too myopic, and too discouraged.

If you offer a monkey one banana now or six bananas later, he will always take the one banana now, says Felix. When many people think like these monkeys and are just interested in making a quick profit, the children of the world have a big problem. They suffer the consequences of the things we cannot fix.

No Money for the Future—Or Just Wearing the Wrong Glasses?

Felix points out in his recent book *Alles würde gut*, that in 2000, the United Nations defined the so-called "millennium development goals" (MDGs). They were supposed to be achieved by 2015. Well, they haven't been. The explanation: not enough money. If you take a closer look, the financial crisis in 2008 and the bailout for the banks that caused the crisis cost several times more than the MDGs would have. The money taxpayers spent on just one German bank would have funded the MDGs globally for a year. (Finkbeiner,2013,10)

Our inaction is expensive, much more so than any action. British economist Nicholas Stern showed as early as 2006 that averting the climate crisis would cost 1 percent of the global GDP. Not doing anything would cost 5 percent. Who is making our calculations? Based on what? And at what cost?

Felix's message has already gone around the world. At the climate conference in Cancun in 2010, children wore T-shirts saying: "You have been debating since before we were born. Don't tell us you need more time!"

"Stop talking. Start planting.": Reaching the Goal in Three Steps

Between 2008 and 2010, the children conducted several global surveys among thousands of children and teenagers from more than one hundred countries. The project had the support of several UN organizations as well as polling institutes in the United States, Europe, and Japan. They condensed the results into four words: "Stop talking. Start planting."

On February 2, 2011, they presented their three-point plan based on these results to the General Assembly of the United Nations.

1. Let Us Plant a Thousand Billion Trees by 2020.

In the last six years, adults and children have already planted more than 12.6 billion trees. Only 987.4 billion to go. Official sources have confirmed that there is enough space, in easily accessible regions around the world, without any impact on agriculture or settlements. Every year, these new trees bind 10 billion tons of manmade CO_2 emissions. This buys us some time to switch to a sustainable CO_2-free lifestyle.

2. Leave the Fossil Fuels in the Earth—Climate Neutrality by 2050

Today, we retrieve as much carbon in the shape of oil, gas, and coal from the earth in a day as the sun deposited there in a million days. The children are calling on the leaders of the world to do what they need to do to achieve 100 percent global climate neutrality by 2050.

3. Fight Poverty with Climate Justice.

The demand: every person in the world gets the same permitted amount of CO_2 emissions. If you need more, you need to pay for it. If a person in Europe wants to emit 10 tons of CO_2 instead of the permitted 1.5 tons, he can buy the right to do it from other people—e.g., in Africa, where people emit only 0.5 tons. People can invest that money in food, education, medical care, and technology.

Are the demands of Felix and the children of the world realistic? And how long would it take? Let's see: 2^{32} = 8 billion. Two people are not many. But if two people convince two other people of an idea, and if these four people convince four others in a month, and so on, all of mankind would be convinced in thirty-two months. Who says it would take too long? In a world where the "Gangnam Style" video got several million clicks in a few days, how long does it take to spread an idea that could save the world?

The underlying question is: Where is our focus? What gets our attention? Since the financial crisis hit, nobody takes climate change seriously anymore. The financial crisis was replaced with the poverty crisis. Then there was the euro crisis—we go from one emergency to the next. Do we really want to wait until we see and feel the consequences of climate change before we start paying attention to it?

So far, Felix and the team of Plant-for-the-Planet have trained seventeen thousand children around the world in one-day workshops in thirty countries to pass on the idea, organize tree planting events, and work for their own future. By 2020, they want to be a million.

Felix's role model is Kenyan Nobel Laureate Professor Wangari Maathai (who died in 2011), who mobilized other women to plant thirty million trees in thirty years and later started the Billion Trees Campaign. She once said: "The little things people do have an effect. This will make the difference in the long run. My little thing is that I plant trees." Thanks to Wangari Maathai, all children in Kenya know that they each have to plant eight trees in their lifetime—or they will breathe someone else's air.

Where are the people who stop talking and start doing? Felix and his team find it rather alarming that the four German nuclear power companies use the term *sustainability* a combined 210 times on their websites. Companies, the kids think, do not need sustainability departments but need to make sustainability their corporate goal. Now. It takes twenty-five years for some of the consequences of our actions or inaction today to become apparent. Who is going to be around then? Certainly Felix and his team.

What Are the Benefits for the Seventh Generation?

Chief Saw told the children about the elder council of a tribe. The council examines all big decisions to determine whether it will still benefit the seventh generation that comes after them.

Felix says: "If we had such a sustainability council, there would be no nuclear power or burning fossil fuels, we wouldn't have all of these financial tools nobody understands and there wouldn't be people speculating with food while others are starving. So far, I haven't met anyone who could explain to us kids why we need speculators."

At the end of our meeting, Felix gives me a Change Chocolate bar. This is good chocolate—and many big German stores already carry it. Plant-for-the-Planet introduced the chocolate in April of 2012. It is an example of how the kids think all products around the world should be: fair-trade and climate-neutral. The cocoa farmers receive enough money that they can plant precious wood between their cocoa trees, thus raising their income from four thousand to twenty thousand US dollars. Now their children can go to school instead of harvesting cocoa beans for us. More than a million chocolate bars sold in Germany in eight months. In addition to the precious timber trees in Ghana, a tree is planted for every five bars sold—that is another 200,000 trees.

Felix is a living example of the values I talked about in this book. We can learn a lot from his initiative, his courage, and his commitment:

- The successful cooperation of young people and elders is important.
- Great things can be achieved with small ideas.
- It is important to have a common vision.
- We need to let go in order to allow things to grow.
- The principle of give-and-take pays off.
- Nature is our most important partner.

A thousand billion trees—150 trees per person. I think it sounds doable and gives hope. It took ten years to get to the moon, so planting some trees should not be that difficult, right? I have already bought the first thousand trees. And I joined FUTURE FEE, an initiative in which companies support Plant-for-the-Planet with 0.1 per mil of their turnover.

I was deeply impressed by the conversation with Felix. It is certainly one of the meetings I will never forget. Felix and his entire team stand for a movement we need desperately right now. Wangari Maathai said: "In the course of history, there comes a time when humanity is called to shift to a new level of consciousness, to reach a higher moral ground. A time when we have to shed our fear and give hope to each other. That time is now."

That time is now. What can your company do? You as a manager? As a person? Where is our contribution for the next seven generations?

The children of the world are showing us how. They have the strength, courage, and mental agility to drive the necessary changes. Let us support them with all we have. Let us take responsibility and leadership—as companies, as parents, as role models for people who have the right to be alive tomorrow.

For more information on the goals and projects of Plant-for-the-Planet, please visit www.plant-for-the-planet.org.

EPILOGUE

TIME FOR BEAUTY, TIME FOR NEW OLD PATHS

On January 12, 2007, star violinist Joshua Bell stood in the subway in Washington, DC, playing a selection of famous pieces of classical music. Only a few people noticed him. Most of the ones who stopped to listen were children, whose stressed-out parents dragged them onward. Joshua Bell, a world-class musician, made thirty-two dollars in forty-five minutes—on a 3.5 million-dollar violin. Two days before his subway performance, he had played in a sold-out concert hall in Boston—average ticket price: one hundred US dollars. When Joshua Bell stopped playing on January 12, nobody noticed. Nobody clapped.

The subway event was an experiment set up by *The Washington Post*. It poses the question: Do we perceive beauty when we encounter it? Do we stop and feel gratitude for this moment? Do we recognize talent in unusual surroundings? And: if we don't even have a moment to stop and listen to one of the world's best musicians playing some of the world's most beautiful music—what else are we missing out on?

I hope that the information and insights in this book will inspire you to discover the beauty in your company, in your tribe, and in yourself as a leader. Discover it, develop it, and hold it close. I hope that my path encourages you to combine the old traditions of our ancestors with new traditions of your own, so that we all can walk together on new old paths.

The Navajo have a prayer that is an integral part of the Beauty Way Ceremony. Here it is:

The Beauty Way
In beauty may I walk
All day long may I walk
Through the returning seasons may I walk
Beautifully I will possess again
Beautifully birds
Beautifully joyful birds
On the trail marked with pollen may I walk
With grasshoppers about my feet may I walk
With dew about my feet may I walk
With beauty may I walk
With beauty before me may I walk
With beauty behind me may I walk
With beauty above me may I walk
With beauty all around me may I walk
In old age, wandering on a trail of beauty, lively, may I walk
In old age, wandering on a trail of beauty, living again,
may I walk
It is finished in beauty
It is finished in beauty.
Anonymous (Navajo)

I wish you beauty wherever you go and whatever you do.
A-ho!
Barbara Wittmann

INTERVIEW WITH THE AUTHOR

You deal quite a bit with the life of the Native Americans. How did that come about?

It began with the books from German writer Karl May. Like many children of my generation, his stories about tribal life and adventures fascinated me—I stuck feathers in my hair and roamed through the woods. I watched all of the films, of course; and as a child, I thought the proud chief's son was quite handsome. There was something majestic about him, proud.

That was your childhood. Often, such interests quickly disappear—not for you?

Well, the purely childish fascination definitely faded to some extent. But nature, which plays a major role for the Native Americans, continued to capture my attention. In my youth, I discovered mountain biking, which brought me to explore the mountains. I loved being outdoors. When I was eighteen years old, I went to California, in the United States, for several months. There, the places that I got to know on my bike became wilder. Something was different there than in the Bavarian forests. There was a tangible sense of another history—a history in which you couldn't get around the topic of Native Americans. It made me feel at home and supported.

Was it this feeling that kept you looking for Jobs with US-based companies throughout your professional career?

Probably—but a lot of that happened unconsciously. For instance, back when I was spending a lot of time in Silicon Valley, I started doing a ritual: on the day before I would leave, I always rode through San Francisco over the Golden Gate Bridge into Mill Valley. Each time, I met a friend there and we went up on Mt. Tam to watch the sunset. That was my way of slowing down after the hectic pace of Silicon Valley. As I learned later on, Mt. Tam is a very significant place in Native American history.

Rituals and special sites also play a key role in your book and your coaching. But back in Bavaria, the "Indian mountain" was missing, wasn't it?

That was painful, but I had trouble in general finding such rituals and special sites when I first started working independently. In the early years, I wasn't able to make frequent trips to America. I had the idea of just buying a teepee for my garden. After a hectic week, I would sit inside it and make a fire—a kind of Bavarian-Indian recharging practice.

Since then, tents and fires have become an important ingredient for nature-based coaching and management.

It's extremely fascinating to me. As soon as I found myself in a teepee, something would happen to me. And this is evidently true for others as well: more and more people would come to me, wanting to sit by the fire. That's where I had my deepest conversations. Later, I included the tent in my coaching work—people open up in a very different way in there. And I wanted to learn more about the secret of this straightforwardness. I read everything I could get my hands on about Native Americans, and I kept stumbling upon the term *vision quest.* It was clear to me: you have to do that! In 2010, I set forth on my first vision quest in Colorado.

Could you explain what a vision quest is and what effect it had on you?

A vision quest basically means that one resorts to certain places in nature and fasts there for a few days. It's a way to pause, to come closer to oneself, to get back to one's essence. Often, it includes contact with medicine men and women in the region. For example, a Navajo medicine woman made a visit to the group during my first fourteen-day trip. She makes sand paintings; that's her healing practice. She also adds a touch of dry humor and always makes wonderful analogies, like when she said: "Many people think that you can order wisdom like a Happy Meal at a drive-through—but life is not a McDonald's." She's a cool woman, so things aren't always so dead serious with her.

Things went pretty quickly for you: two years after your first vision quest, you began training as a vision-quest guide. What started you off?

During the two weeks of my first vision quest, my life changed in a fundamental way: I became more whole as a human being. It was a personal experience of getting things in order and finding clarity about what I want and who I am. I learned more about my essence. I was so excited about how much can happen in such a short time that in 2012, I decided to train with the School of Lost Borders in California to become a vision-quest guide. Another decisive influence was a fateful experience at the deathbed of a friend. She was a vision-quest guide and had guided me on my first journey. It was her last wish that I continue on this path and work to build bridges. That last conversation had a deep effect on me. Since that time, I've started to guide groups into the inner- and outer wilderness. In my courses for becoming a council trainer, I work together with a mentor. She shares the age-old knowledge with me in trust that I will carry on the tradition.

What role have vision quests played in your life since that time?

For me, it's become a core part of my life: once a year, I go into the wilderness to my personal retreat spot and fast. I see myself as a lifelong learner. With every one of these experiences and every encounter with old teachings, I learn more about myself. That includes the belief that everyone in this world has a unique talent to contribute. My experiences allow me to further uncover my own talent. They have made me a better coach, better able to support others. With each of these experiences, my ego has gotten smaller. That makes more room for other things: humility, trust, grace, and gratitude.

What is one of these days in the wilderness like?

Truly unspectacular. I let myself drift; I have no pressure, no particular distances to cover, and no deadlines. It's very liberating! Most of the time, I sleep under the stars. I don't bring a tent, just a tarp that protects me in bad weather. I carry everything I need on my back; it's an extraordinary feeling of freedom. While I'm packing, I realize how little is truly important. When I guide groups on vision quests, it's always interesting to see how much people lug around with them. An over-packed rucksack is a mirror for life. I try to leave more and more behind. No telephone, no e-mails—just nature and me. During the first few days, my thoughts are still racing, until, at a certain point, it gets very quiet and I can finally hear the important things. Then, I have time to reflect and to simply enjoy my life, health, and freedom.

And how is it coming back home?

Going from this slowed-down, minimalistic situation back into my daily life of corporate consulting is always hard; it's a bit surreal, as well, during the first few days. I'm not immune to the call of the hamster wheel, either. At that time, it's important for me to have my set rituals in order to vitalize my experience despite the hectic pace. It's also important to have discipline and integrity in my relationship with myself. I don't understand at all why some people are afraid of being alone in nature. For me, it's a safer place. In nature, if I keep my eyes open, dangers present themselves very directly, and I have time to react. I often miss that when I come back. In the conference room, the snake doesn't rattle before it bites—the attack comes without warning. I prefer the wilderness in nature to the wilderness in business. For me, it's important to plan brief time-outs so that what I've experienced—my essence—doesn't get lost in everyday life.

What form do these time-outs take?

I keep one weekend per month free—time just for myself. Then, I go hiking or I go to a beautiful place in nature. I leave the computer at home. I cultivate my own liberty, clarify my senses, and recharge. I apply a lot of what I've learned in the wilderness to my daily business life: reduce dead weight; carry as little baggage as possible. That can be applied to work as well as to private life. The less dead weight we have, the more freely we breathe. Many things that I learn when I'm alone in nature first begin to make sense when I have a bit of distance. A major realization can come in the middle of a business meeting, and a seemingly insignificant moment in nature can lead to a flash of insight.

How would your life have gone if these turning points and experiences hadn't taken place?

I would have probably ended up in a burnout clinic. More than once in my professional career, I have been at the brink of a breakdown. It's as if "faster, higher, farther" was written in the small print on my business card. But I was always able to get myself together just before things fell apart because certain turns of fate in my environment, like the death of my friend, always allowed me to take a break. Ever since, I have been living more intensely, taking my dreams more seriously, and daring to do things that push me out of my comfort zone—for instance, writing a book and making my convictions public.

Your book also deals with contemporary Western society. What's going wrong?

Our world works in terms of extremes: poor/rich, young/old, stress/relaxation, and war/peace. We've lost our center as human beings and as a society. "Work/life balance" is a catchphrase of our times—I don't stand behind that. Balance implies a relationship between two poles. But this approach doesn't lead to the goal because every circle and cycle has a center. Only when we begin to move in cycles again, when we begin to take nature as a role model and stop indiscriminately destroying it can we find our center again.

How can this topic be communicated to executives without it seeming too esoteric?

The word *esoteric* raises the hair on my neck. For me, that's the worst buzzword of our times. It was introduced with good intentions, and in the meantime, it's developed a strange aftertaste. *Esoteric* makes me think of people who spend all their time floating on a cloud and are completely detached from life. I'm far from that, because I'd like to communicate something very rooted. The term that I prefer to use is *naturalness.* It's something that we've lost. For me, *naturalness* means a relationship to the nature around us and within us. In the West, that is the essence of all the teachings of our ancestors, whether Indians or the primal Bavarians. The Indians took nature as their model. From nature, they learned the meaning of living in a cycle. Take the Indian medicine wheel: it gives us countless lessons. It's profound and multilayered; one can study it for an entire lifetime. I communicate these universal lessons in a simple way, a way that makes them understandable for everyone. It's part of our nature, and it just wants to be brought back into our lives.

Can you give an example?

When I talk with managers, I have a simple analogy for the medicine wheel: the saying "work hard; play hard!" I also followed this principle for a long time—for example, first lots of brain work, then extreme sports. In terms of the medicine wheel, that's the North and the South. In between is fire. It's said that whoever jumps over the fire will get burned. It would be better if we once more respected all of the cardinal directions. That would mean bringing dreams and gratitude back into our lives. This gives many people a eureka moment because almost everyone has forgotten their dreams, lost their sense of gratitude. That's just a tiny sliver of what's possible.

How do your examples and analogies lead to real changes for the people you coach?

I think that it really becomes possible when people see that it's not just about empty catchphrases. The world has had enough of those. Managers and executives are tired of running after the next management trend. What I communicate doesn't come from me, but from something that belongs to all of us and wants to be brought back into our lives. I'm just an intermediary; the real coach is nature. That message is extremely well received. People are able to achieve so much through very simple, small things. For example, readers of my book tell me that they have started doing regular medicine walks. Or that they are able to learn so much when they move through nature with open eyes. Small steps toward slowing down, bit by bit freeing one's own naturalness. I'm happy to be the modern coaching midwife for that process. But every person has to live it for him- or herself.

How could this principle be applied to families?

Instead of sitting in front of the television or the Xbox, it would be enough to sit down now and again at a table together for meals. To really talk with one another. Many children, as well as many adults, lack the experience of being seen and heard. If people would once again pay more attention to that, it would already be a major step. Or telling stories, having adventures together, maybe roasting a sausage over the campfire. Anything that supports sharing and understanding would be good. That neither costs a lot of money nor takes a lot of time.

How is your work with women and men different?

Women are more open to group work. That makes it possible to do much more as a community, and more exchange takes place than does with men. Problems are more often discussed. Men, on the other hand, read my book and are deeply moved but don't admit it openly. If we delve into any topics, it takes place in individual coaching.

What's in store for the future? Are there any new plans?

For next year, I plan to give talks and readings. In the autumn, there will be a leadership quest, which is a vision quest for executives. There are already ideas for the next book project. Alongside all of these activities, I will be attending to my companies. For me, it's a matter of finding a good balance between what is and what will be.

In one sentence: What makes life beautiful for you?

Loving myself—and loving what I do.

ABOUT THE AUTHOR

Barbara Wittmann is a consultant, coach, and CEO of three companies mostly in the field of IT. Since 2006, she has supported teams and projects as a coach during change processes. She solves tricky IT issues and gets projects that have veered off course back on the right track. She also supports people and companies in developing and living their full potential.

In our technology-driven world, we often neglect the human factor. Therefore, Barbara trained as a team and group coach (organizational relationship coaching, ORSC) and earned her qualification as a Co-Active Coach at the Coaches Training Institute.

In order to hone her senses and keep her own visions alive, she travels regularly to the sacred places of Native Americans in the United States to experience the wilderness.

She attended classes at the Animas Valley Institute (AVI) in Colorado, where she learned how to use her experiences in nature to support personal development. At the School of Lost Borders in California, she trained as a rites of passage guide. She is currently on the path of council trainer to learn more about the power of story and circle.

As a passionate entrepreneur, she knows about the power of visions and dreams—and how difficult the path can be, if they are lacking. She recognizes that her companies can grow only if she grows as a person and that she can motivate her employees and clients only if she lives her own values and principles.

Visit www.barbarawittmann.de to learn more.

FURTHER READING

Campbell, Joseph: *The Power of Myth*, Anchor, 1991.

Foster, Steven and Meredith Little: *Book of Vision Quest*, Touchstone, 1989.

Foster, Steven, and Meredith Little: *The Four Shields: The Initiatory Seasons of Human Nature*, Lost Borders Press, 1999.

Godin, Seth: *Tribes, We Need You to Lead Us*, Do You Zoom, Inc., 2008.

Hallowell, Edward M.: *Shine: Using Brain Science to Get the Best from Your People*, 2011.

Jensen, Rolf: *The Dream Society: How the Coming Shift from Information to Imagination Will Transform Your Business*, McGraw-Hill, 1999.

Johnson, Flynn: *Journey to the Sacred Mountains*, Findhorn Press

Loehr, Jim: *The Power of Story*, Free Press, a Division of Simon & Schuster, NY

Manz, Charles C.: *The Leadership Wisdom of Jesus: Practical Lessons for Today*, Berret Koehler, 1999.

Marshall III, Joseph M.: *Keep Going*, Sterling Ethos, 2009.

Nickerson, Kern, and Walking Thunder: *Walking Thunder: Diné Medicine Woman,* Leete's Island Books, 2001.

Plotkin, Bill: *Soulcraft: Crossing into the Mysteries of Nature and Psyche*, New World Library, 2003.

Plotkin, Bill: *Nature and the Human Soul*, New World Library, 2007.

Schaefer, Carol: *Grandmothers Counsel the World: Women Elders Offer Their Vision for Our Planet*, Trumpeter, 2006.

Senge, Peter M.: *The Fifth Discipline*, Doubleday, 2006.

Storm, Hyemeyohsts: *Seven Arrows*, Ballantine Books, 1985.

Surowiecki, James: *The Wisdom of Crowds*, Currency Books/ Doubleday, a Division of Random House, Inc., 2004.

Zimmermann, Jack, and Virginia Coyl: *The Way of Council*, Bramble Books, 2009.

BIBLIOGRAPHY

Gunn Allen, Paula: *The Sacred Hoop: Recovering the Feminine in American Indian Traditions.* Beacon Press, 1992

Finkbeiner, Felix: *Alles würde gut.* Self published by Plant-for-the-Planet, 2013

Manjoo, Fahrhad: *The Happiness Machine, How Google became such a great place to work*, Slate Magazine, Januar 2013, http://www.slate.com/articles/technology/technology/2013/01/google_people_operations_the_secrets_of_the_world_s_most_scientific_human.html

Printed in the United States
By Bookmasters